I0223749

TARIFFS TANTRUMS AND TRADE WARS

HOW TO SOURCE, SELL AND STAY PROFITABLE WHEN GLOBAL TRADE GETS NASTY

DONOVAN GARETT

Copyright © 2025 AlgoRhythms Studios, Ltd. All rights reserved.

Any attempt to reproduce, translate and/or distribute in any form any part of this work beyond that permitted by Section 107 or 108 of the 1976 United States Copyright Act without express written consent by the copyright owner is illegal. No part of this publication may be duplicated, stored in a retrieval system, or transmitted in any form or by any means electronic, mechanical, photocopied, recorded or otherwise, without the prior written permission of the publisher. Requests for permission or further information can be sent by U.S. mail at the following address:

AlgoRhythms Studios, Ltd.

P.O. BOX 35643

Cleveland, Ohio 44135

United States of America

DISCLAIMER. This publication is intended (but not guaranteed) to provide accurate information in regard to the subject matter covered. Some information may not be applicable to every reader or every situation. It is sold with the understanding that neither the author, publisher, nor any other person or entity connected with the creation, publication, or distribution of this publication provides legal, accounting, logistics, or other professional services. If expert assistance is required, the services of a competent professional should be sought.

PRINT ISBN: 978-1-963267-35-8

E-BOOK ISBN: 978-1-963267-36-5

Library of Congress Control Number: 2025912081

Printed in the United States of America

Contents

Restructure Your Value Chain – "Local First"

U.S. / Mexico / Canada Nearshoring

Build a Trade-Resilient Brand

Prepare for the Next Trade War Now

The Final Takeaway:

Stay Lean. Stay Local. Stay Ready.

Chapter 1

Here We Go . . . Again

As someone with experience importing products from all over the world, I could hardly believe what I was seeing on the news. With one stroke of a pen, the U.S. imposed tariffs of 10% on Chinese-made goods.

. . . 10% eventually turns into 34%.

. . . 34% eventually turns into 104%

. . . 104% eventually turns into 125%, then 145%, then 245%.

Wow. Really? . . .

At that point, I simply turned off the news and started working on this book. I knew that small business owners could use something actually *"helpful,"* instead of watching trade tensions steadily escalate into full-blown global logistics chaos.

If you listen closely, you can hear the constant sound of *"sabre-rattling"* as it echoes through the air. It's early spring, 2025. It feels as though the official U.S. policy toward global trade is to *"shoot first . . . and keep shooting."*

Trade conflicts between the U.S. and China are nothing new, but have now evolved into ongoing battles of political will that continue to reshape the future of global commerce. As of April 2025, the situation has escalated significantly. The latest tariff increases now target a broad range of imports, placing added pressure on small businesses already reeling from COVID-era inflation and that rely heavily on global supply chains.

Tariff hikes don't occur in a vacuum. In response, China has expanded its own trade restrictions. Retaliatory tariffs now apply to a wide range of U.S. goods. However, in a powerful show of defiance, China has stopped buying billions of dollars worth of U.S. agricultural products, including soybeans and corn, choosing to purchase from countries such as Brazil, effectively leaving U.S. farmers to wonder whether they will remain solvent through this trade crisis. Additionally, Chinese regulatory agencies have increased inspections and compliance requirements for imports, further slowing the flow of goods.

The ripple effects are clear. Shipping costs have surged due to capacity shortages and port congestion. Customs delays are growing more frequent, and businesses are experiencing inconsistent clearance times, especially for mixed or component-based shipments. Even routine deliveries are being held up because of stricter scrutiny and longer inspection windows at ports of entry.

The cost of doing business with overseas suppliers has climbed across the board—tariffs, freight, time, and geopolitical uncertainty. As a small business owner, you no doubt realize first-hand that this isn't some abstract logistics theory, or a foreign policy issue restricted to news headlines. These problems are daily operational challenges that threaten profitability, delivery timelines, and erode customer trust.

U.S.-China trade relations have entered a new phase, which, naturally, requires a new strategy. If your business depends on Chinese imports, now is the time to realistically assess your exposure, tighten your supply chain, and begin shifting toward more stable, domestic alternatives. Waiting for things to just *"settle down"* is no longer a viable plan.

Why Small Businesses Take the Biggest Hit

Tariffs don't impact all businesses equally. Large corporations often have the leverage, resources, and internal infrastructure to absorb or deflect the added costs, or even quickly pivot trade routes to more tariff–friendly jurisdictions. Small businesses, on the other hand, cannot afford that luxury. When tariffs increase, it's the smallest players—those with limited bargaining power, thin margins, and less room to maneuver—who are impacted most.

The first and most obvious pressure point is landed cost.[1] Small businesses must either absorb the higher expenses or pass them on to customers when import duties rise. Unlike large firms with diversified supplier bases and the power to negotiate bulk pricing, smaller operations generally depend on a single overseas vendor for critical products or components. That dependency results in exposure, leaving them unable to renegotiate terms or switch sources quickly.

Next is cash flow. Higher upfront costs for goods, longer shipping times, and unexpected delays all stretch finances thinner. Products that once took 30 days to arrive may now take twice as long, tying up capital in transit while demand continues to shift. Today, in 2025, many small businesses are paying more for inventory that arrives later and sells more slowly than in 2024.

The issue also extends to supply chain fragility. With fewer resources, most small companies lack dedicated procurement teams, logistics analysts, or compliance experts. This makes it harder to respond quickly to customs changes, documentation

---

1. Landed cost is the total cost of getting a product from the factory to a customer's door. It includes shipping fees, insurance, and any customs and duties due if the goods cross borders. Source: https://www.dhl.com/discover/en-global/logistics-advice/essential-guides/landed-cost-meaning-formula-calculation

rules, or inspection delays. When one part of the supply chain fails, small businesses often lack a solid contingency plan needed to keep operations running smoothly.

Most importantly, there's a hidden cost in customer experience. When inventory is late or unavailable, customers don't blame international trade policy—they blame the business in front of them. Late shipments, shortages, and price hikes lead to negative reviews, lost loyalty, and reputational damage that is difficult to recover from. Larger competitors, with more inventory and greater supply chain flexibility, are generally able to maintain consistency, or even gain political leverage where small businesses cannot.

In short, global trade disruptions create a perfect storm for small business owners: rising costs, longer delays, limited options, and higher expectations. The combination leaves little room for error. That's why building resilience into your supply chain is a necessity.

This Isn't a Trade Dispute—It's a Wake-Up Call

For decades, business owners viewed tariffs as a proverbial *"pebble in the shoe"*—a minor irritation caused by political chatter that would eventually fade into obscurity. That mindset is no longer viable. The current trade challenges are not minor setbacks. They are a new operating reality. The U.S.-China tariff conflict has mushroomed into a paradigm shift in how global commerce functions, and businesses that continue waiting for it to disappear are falling behind.

Current events aren't simply about economics. They're about strategy. The global supply chain has become a fragile system, vulnerable to sudden policy shifts, geopolitical tensions, and unpredictable enforcement at every stage—from raw materials to final delivery. The margin for error has all but evaporated for small businesses that rely on fast turnarounds and price consistency.

Companies that thrive in this new landscape are not necessarily the biggest or the cheapest—they're the most adaptable. Waiting for policy or trade agreements to change, hoping for tariff relief, or sticking with unreliable suppliers out of habit are no longer acceptable business practices. They are risks. And unmanaged risks often have severe consequences.

Here's What You'll Learn . . .

I'm writing this book because I truly felt the need to give small business owners something more. More than just dry logistics theory or economic posturing. You need answers. Real answers that allow you to take immediate action.

In this book, you'll learn how to audit your current supply chain to find vulnerabilities you may not even know exist. We'll walk through how to break down your product lines, identify where your dependencies lie, and pinpoint the areas where tariffs, shipping delays, or raw material shortages could cause the most damage.

You'll get a step-by-step guide on how to find domestic manufacturers and suppliers that work with small businesses, not just large enterprise buyers. You'll learn the tools and platforms that connect you directly with American producers—no middlemen, no guesswork.

You'll also learn how to protect your margins without sacrificing quality or losing customers. That includes smarter pricing strategies, stronger vendor negotiations, and strategies to shift your product mix without derailing your brand equity or customer experience.

As the landscape continues to shift, I'll show you how to rethink your product strategy—what to stop selling, what to redesign, and how to rely less on high-risk imports and more on sustainable, flexible options.

Finally, we'll discuss building long-term resilience—not just surviving one crisis, but being in a position to thrive regardless of where the next disruption comes from. Whether it's a tariff hike, a shipping slowdown, or another supply chain shock, you'll be able to respond with clarity and confidence.

So . . . If you're running a product-based business and watching your margins shrink, your freight costs spike, or your orders show up late—or not at all . . . Or, If you own a business in e-commerce, retail, wholesale, or light manufacturing and you're feeling the weight of tariffs, raw material shortages, and supplier instability, this book will help you take back control.

Even if you're not directly importing from China, but your vendors are—this book will show you how to uncover risks and navigate around them.

I'm thrilled and honored to be a part of your journey.

Let's begin.

Chapter 2

How We Got Here

B efore you can protect your business from tariffs, you need to understand what they are, how they work, and why this particular trade conflict isn't just another policy change—it's a fundamental, structural shift with long-term consequences.

This chapter provides a no-nonsense breakdown of the U.S. -China tariff war and what it means for you as a small business owner. You'll learn how tariffs function, how we got to this point, and why the current escalation (as of early Spring 2025) is different from what we've seen in the past.

You'll also get a clear picture of why shipping delays, customs bottlenecks, and soaring freight costs are no longer just symptoms of pandemic recovery—they're part of a larger, more permanent realignment of global trade.

Let's start with the basics—what tariffs really are, and why they've likely become the single biggest external threat to your supply chain.

What Tariffs Are and How They Work

Simply put, a tariff is a tax. When a product crosses a border into the United States, and that product is subject to a tariff, the importer—the business bringing the goods in—has to pay that tax before the goods are released into the country.

Not the foreign manufacturer.

Not the exporter.

You, the buyer, pay it.

That distinction matters. Many business owners assume tariffs are penalties on the exporting country. They're not. They're direct costs forced on your business—costs you either absorb or pass on to your customers.

Tariffs are calculated as a percentage of the product's value, and that's not the only expense. You also have to pay freight charges, insurance, customs handling, and port fees. Once it's all added up, the actual landed cost of a product can be significantly higher than expected, sometimes 20%, 30%, or more.

What really matters here is how those costs quietly erode your profit margins. They don't show up on your customer's invoice right away. In fact, they start to add up long before the product even reaches store shelves. That makes every sourcing decision more critical, every quote more fragile, and every pricing adjustment more strategic.

There are several types of tariffs, but the ones affecting most U.S. small businesses fall into three basic categories:

Ad Valorem Tariffs – Charged as a percentage of the item's value. Used to raise revenue, protect a country's domestic industry, or regulate trade.

Specific Tariffs – Flat-rate fees based on quantity or weight, regardless of value.

Safeguard or Retaliatory Tariffs – Increases used as leverage in political disputes. Safeguard tariffs are generally imposed to protect a domestic industry from injury caused by a surge in imports, while retaliatory tariffs are imposed in response to tariffs imposed by another country.

As of the time of writing this book, the bulk of the pressure is coming from *ad valorem* tariffs, especially on Chinese imports. These apply across thousands of categories—consumer electronics, raw materials, industrial parts, textiles, tools—and they stack up quickly.

This is where many small businesses get caught off guard. Tariffs don't just make things more expensive—they introduce volatility into every layer of your business. Invoices shift. Supplier quotes expire faster. Shipping becomes harder to predict. And if you're not actively monitoring your exposure, the impact can go unnoticed until it's too late to respond.

> ***Key Takeaway:*** Understanding how tariffs function gives you leverage. Once you recognize how these hidden costs operate, you can start taking steps to reduce your dependency and build a more stable path forward.

A Brief History of U.S.—China Trade Conflicts

To understand where we are today, you need to understand how we got here. The current tariff war between the United States and China didn't begin overnight. It's the result of decades of tension, rooted in trade imbalances, intellectual property disputes, national security concerns, and the growing rivalry between two economic superpowers.

Since China joined the World Trade Organization in December, 2001, U.S. imports from China have surged. American businesses—large and small—benefited from low-cost labor, mass production capacity, and the ability to scale rapidly. In most cases, sourcing from China became the *de-facto* operating model.

Beneath the surface, however, cracks began to form. The U. S. trade deficit with China has ballooned year after year over several decades. American officials have long accused Chinese firms of flooding the market with underpriced goods, engaging in state-sponsored industrial espionage, and using forced technology transfers for market access.

The tipping point came in 2018, when the U.S. began imposing tariffs on hundreds of Chinese products, citing national security concerns and unfair trade practices. China responded in kind. What followed was a rapid back-and-forth cycle of tariffs, threats, negotiations, and retaliations—each side layering new restrictions and countermeasures in a slow-moving but relentless escalation.

At first, many small business owners assumed the conflict would be resolved quickly—just another round of political posturing. However, as the trade war continued into 2019, 2020, and beyond, it became clear this was more than just a policy spat. It was the beginning of a long-term restructuring of global trade.

The Current Landscape — Spring, 2025

As of early Spring, 2025, the U.S.-China trade war has intensified, with both nations imposing significant tariffs on each other's goods. The United States has escalated its tariffs on Chinese imports, while China has responded with its own set of retaliatory measures.

The U.S. has imposed a 145% tariff on Chinese imports, affecting a wide range of products, including consumer electronics, textiles, machinery, and raw materials like steel and aluminum.

In response, China has implemented a 125% tariff on U.S. goods and has strategically halted imports of Agricultural products such as soybeans and corn, as well as large industrial products like Boeing aircraft, significantly impacting critical U.S. industries such as Aerospace.

Heightened tariffs have contributed to increased shipping costs and delays. Port congestion remains a significant issue, with approximately 8.4% of the global container fleet delayed due to ongoing port congestion.[1] Major ports in Asia, Latin America, and North America, especially on the U.S. West Coast, are still facing heavy backlogs, with vessels waiting up to 14–21 days.[2]

These developments have placed additional strain on small businesses, already reeling from inflation, who often lack the resources to absorb increased costs or navigate complex international logistics. The combination of higher tariffs, shipping delays, and supply chain disruptions necessitates a reevaluation

---

1. https://www.vizionapi.com/blog/port-issues-congestion-trends-north-america

2. https://www.chrobinson.com/en-us/resources/insights-and-advisories/north-america-freight-insights/mar-2025-freight-market-update/key-freight-service-updates/ocean/

of sourcing strategies and supply chain management for small business owners.

Why Businesses Must Pivot Now

The U.S.-China trade conflict has escalated beyond tariffs, with China now leveraging its dominance in critical materials as a strategic tool. On April 4, 2025, Beijing imposed export restrictions on several rare earth minerals, essential for various high-tech and defense applications.

At this point, it's clear that tariffs are no longer a temporary friction point—they've become part of the permanent cost structure of global trade. Waiting for things to return to "normal" is not only unrealistic—it's dangerous. While political shifts might lead to future negotiations, the direction of policy is clear: both the U.S. and China are doubling down on economic nationalism, self-reliance, and strategic protectionism.

The risk isn't just higher costs—it's operational paralysis. Businesses that rely heavily on overseas suppliers are already seeing longer lead times, more frequent shortages, and fluctuating price quotes that make economic forecasting nearly impossible. And it's incredibly difficult to recover once margins collapse or customer trust is lost.

The smart move here is based on speed. Not panic. Not overreaction. Just planful, deliberate action before you're forced to react under pressure. Businesses that win in this climate aren't the ones with the most resources. They're the ones with the clearest visibility, the fastest pivots, and the best preparation.

Chapter 3

How Tariffs Hurt Small Businesses

Tariffs may look like a policy issue from the outside, but inside your business, they hit where it matters most—what I like to refer to as *"the three c's"*: cost, cash flow, and customer confidence. While large corporations can cushion much of the impact with bulk buying, multiple sourcing contracts, and entire departments dedicated to navigating global trade, small businesses don't have that kind of buffer.

For small business owners, every shipment matters. Every supplier relationship counts. Every dollar spent on inventory, freight, and customs comes directly out of working capital. The effects are immediate and compounding when tariffs increase, even by a few percentage points. You pay more for the same products, wait longer for them to arrive, and lose pricing flexibility at the worse possible time—when your customers are most sensitive to change.

In this chapter, we'll break down specific ways tariffs and trade restrictions tighten the squeeze on small businesses. We'll look at how rising costs eat into margins, how logistics delays are a source of lost revenue, and why customer backlash is an often-overlooked consequence of global instability.

Let's start with the biggest measurable impact: higher costs and lower margins.

Rising Costs and Sinking Profits

Tariffs don't just raise prices—they put added pressure on your entire business model. As a small business owner, costs and budgets are already strained. Margins are thin, overhead is often fixed, and inventory decisions must be precise. So when tariffs are introduced or rapidly fluctuate, they don't just nibble at profits—they take a huge bite.

Let's begin with the most obvious costs: the cost of goods. If a product you used to import at $10 per unit now costs you $12 or more after tariffs, that's a 20% jump. Even *before* you factor in shipping, packaging, printing, or customs clearance fees. If you're ordering in bulk, these amounts multiply quickly across your entire inventory.

The problem isn't just the added cost. It's the unpredictability. It is often stated that tariff uncertainty is more dangerous than the tariffs themselves. As we have all seen, tariff schedules can change with little notice. Political negotiations, trade announcements, or retaliatory actions can shift your prices literally overnight. That makes it nearly impossible to project reliable margins or lock in pricing for long-term customer contracts. You're forced to either eat the cost or pass it on—and both choices can have serious financial repercussions.

This often creates a domino effect. Higher landed costs mean:

Less cash *available for marketing, staffing, or expansion.*

Tighter reorder windows *due to limited working capital.*

More pressure to *raise prices**, which may push customers away to competitors.*

Greater risk of accumulating *slow-moving inventory* *that no longer justify its profit margin.*

Key Takeaway: What truly matters here is that financial pressure doesn't stop at the port of entry. If your margins erode by even 5–10%, it can be the difference between growth and stagnation—or worse.

The ultimate goal isn't to eliminate cost pressure. That's not even remotely feasible in this trade climate. It's to identify where your biggest vulnerabilities lie and build strategies to protect your profit margins before they vanish completely.

Delays, Disruptions & Supply-Chain Instability

Even if you're willing to pay more for the goods you import, that doesn't guarantee you'll get them on time—or at all. One of the most frustrating realities of doing business during a global trade conflict is that reliability disappears when you need it most.

Tariffs don't just add cost—they trigger ripple effects throughout the entire logistics chain. Customs authorities are now inspecting shipments more thoroughly, especially those coming from China. If your products or parts are on a flagged list or fall under a high-risk tariff category, expect delays. Documentation errors, even minor ones, can cause containers to be held at the port for days or weeks. In some cases, entire shipments can be rerouted, reassessed, or returned.

Then there's freight. Shipping container costs—after briefly stabilizing after the pandemic—are rising again due to capacity shortages, fuel volatility, and port congestion. Delays hit small businesses the hardest because you don't have the leverage to push your shipment to the front of the line for containers, or the extra funds to pay for air freight.

This is where many small businesses lose control of the situation. They plan for a 30-day turnaround, but it becomes 45 or 60. They may order based on projected demand, but by the time the shipment arrives, the opportunity is gone—or worse, the customer has already gone elsewhere.

This isn't simply a loss of time. It's also a loss of:

Predictability *in cash flow and inventory.*

Credibility *with customers and vendors.*

Agility *in responding to market changes.*

Opportunity *for repeat sales due to inconsistent stock levels.*

A late shipment can mean missed seasonal windows, cancelled contracts, or the inability to fulfill orders during peak periods. This is why supplier reliability and transit predictability have become just as important as price. The cheapest option doesn't matter if it doesn't arrive.

The strategy here is simple: prioritize supply chain stability over short-term savings. That might mean sourcing products closer to home, working with multiple vendors, or building in more lead time than you're used to—but it will protect you when others are stuck waiting for shipments to arrive from overseas.

Cash Flow Challenges

Many small business owners forget that tariffs and shipping delays don't just affect profit margins—they lock up precious cash. Cash is the oxygen that keeps businesses moving forward.

When lead times stretch, it creates a serious timing problem: *money goes out long before revenue comes back in.*

That gap puts pressure on inventory management, payroll, rent, marketing, and even the ability to serve new customers.

When this happens, what used to be predictable is now volatile. That comfortable restocking rhythm? Gone. Now you'll pay more, wait longer, and hope the shipment clears customs without issue. Meanwhile, precious capital is tied up—sitting in a container you can't touch, sell, or even track reliably.

At this point, many small business owners tighten their cash in all the wrong places:

Cutting inventory and risking shortages.

Ending marketing campaigns because inventory can't be guaranteed.

Pausing growth opportunities due to uncertainty.

More importantly, you may be forced to rethink pricing—quickly. But raising prices isn't a switch you can flip on and off without consequence. Customers are very sensitive to price hikes, especially during a recession when competitors are undercutting you or when their trust in your fulfillment timeline is already shaky.

So what do most small businesses do? They hesitate. They wait. They hope things just *"level out."* But the reality is, your cash flow will continue to suffer until you rebuild your sourcing and pricing model around today's market conditions—not yesterday's assumptions.

Smart businesses treat cash flow as a strategic asset, not just a financial outcome. They restructure their purchasing cycles. They renegotiate payment terms. They raise prices where necessary with messaging that communicates reciprocal value, not just price changes.

Customer Backlash and Brand Risk

Tariffs aren't limited to supply chains. They have the power to create serious customer trust issues.

When prices go up, your delivery windows stretch, or your top-selling products suddenly disappear, your customers don't care about trade policy—they blame you. They don't see the customs forms, the import duties, or the shipping delays. They see higher price tags, out-of-stock notifications, or delayed orders.

This is where long-term reputation damage can start to fester. Even if you're doing everything right behind the scenes—paying more for freight, expediting shipments, or absorbing costs to keep pricing steady—none of that matters if the customer experience takes a hit.

 **Key Takeaway:** If you don't communicate proactively with customers during a crisis, they assume the worst: that your business is disorganized, unreliable, or no longer worth their loyalty.

Most commonly, customers express their dissatisfaction quietly with:

Negative reviews about delays or pricing.

*Increased product **returns** or order **cancellations.***

*Lower **repeat purchase** rates.*

Fewer referrals and weaker word-of-mouth advertising.

Silent churn—they just stop buying without telling you why.

To combat this, focus on transparency and consistency. You can't always shield your customers from the impact of global trade issues, but you can explain, communicate, and reinforce the value you're still providing. A well-timed email or website notice that says, *"Here's what's changing and why"* goes a long way. So does training your customer-facing staff to explain product changes without sounding defensive, evasive or vague.

Being honest and responsive (instead of reactive and defensive) will keep more customers during a price hike than hiding behind silence. Customers will forgive a delay—they won't forgive being blindsided.

Remember that in times of uncertainty, human nature is to crave consistency. If you can't offer that in product availability, offer it in service, communication, and professionalism. That's what builds brand resilience—and it's what gives your business a competitive edge when others are crumbling under the pressure.

In the next chapter, we'll shift from identifying problems to building your action plan—starting with how to audit your supply chain and reduce your risk exposure, one step at a time.

Chapter 4

How to Protect and Insulate Your Business

U p to this point, we've talked about how tariffs and trade disruptions affect your margins, your cash flow, your supply chain, and your customer relationships. Now it's time to shift gears—from awareness to action.

This chapter is where you start to regain control.

You don't need to overhaul your business overnight. But what you do need is a structured, strategic approach to reduce your exposure, protect your profits, and build resilience into your daily operations. The tools exist. The suppliers are out there. The opportunity to stabilize and reposition your business is real, and it starts with taking a hard look at where you're vulnerable.

We'll begin with a supply chain audit—something every business, regardless of size, should complete at least once per year. You'll learn how to identify your most at-risk products, evaluate your current vendors, and flag the parts of your process most likely to break under pressure.

Then we'll move into strategy: how to shift toward domestic or diversified sourcing without destroying your cost structure. You'll see how to secure better terms, find reliable suppliers closer to home, and reduce lead times with smarter planning.

Finally, we'll cover pricing strategy and customer messaging. No matter how well you adjust behind the scenes, it won't matter if your customer experience breaks down.

Find Out Where You're Most Vulnerable

Before you can protect your business against trade disruptions, you need to know exactly where it's exposed. And for most small businesses, that exposure starts within your supply chain.

Tariffs, shipping delays, and regulatory slowdowns aren't limited to one region. Sure, countries with punitive tariff rates—such as China—are a major concern, but they're not the only risk. Global trade has become more volatile everywhere. If you're supplying goods from any nation facing heightened trade restrictions or customs scrutiny, you're carrying more risk than you think.

A supply chain audit shouldn't create more complexity—it should help you gain clarity. You need a complete picture of where your products, parts, and materials come from, and which ones are vulnerable to cost spikes, compliance issues, or delays.

Here's a 3-step process to identify potential risks:

Step 1: Audit Your Product List

Start by reviewing your current list of products.

Ask yourself:

- *Which SKUs are sourced from high-risk countries or routed through tariff-heavy regions?*

- *Which items have higher costs, longer lead times, or unpredictable shipping windows?*

- *Which of these products are central to your core revenue stream or customer retention?*

Step 2: Audit Your Vendor List

Next, review your vendor relationships:

- *Are you relying on one supplier for critical products or inputs?*

- *Do you know where your supplier is sourcing from? Have they shifted operations to another region without telling you?*

- *Are any of your vendors passing through third party*

countries to avoid direct tariffs—and if so, are the costs and lead times worth the trade-off?

Step 3: Audit Your Logistics Process

Now, look at your logistics and fulfillment process:

- *Are your products routed through regions experiencing port congestion or customs backlogs?*

- *How often are you dealing with clearance delays, surprise fees, or rebooking issues?*

- *Do you have buffer stock or alternate sourcing routes in place?*

The purpose of this audit is to remove guesswork. A single supplier in a tariff-heavy region could be putting a large portion of your revenue at risk. A delayed container could lock up thousands in cash flow for weeks. What you need is visibility, because once you know where the vulnerabilities are, you can start planning around them.

Source Domestically
Without Breaking the Bank

Over the past few decades, the news media, pop culture, and financial gurus have constantly reinforced the message that "Made in the U.S.A." no longer exists. This simply isn't true. Domestic manufacturing does exist. But the sad truth is, we've just been conditioned to ignore it or assume it's always cost-prohibitive when compared to other countries.

As global trade becomes increasingly fragile, one of the best ways to reduce supply chain risk is to shorten it. That usually means sourcing closer to home. But you probably think the idea of switching to domestic suppliers sounds expensive, complicated, and disruptive.

It doesn't have to be.

Understand that domestic sourcing isn't an all-or-nothing decision. You don't need to replace every overseas vendor or double your unit costs overnight. The secret lies in making targeted shifts—starting with your most vulnerable or high-value products—and building from there.

Start by identifying your highest-risk imports:

- *Products sourced from countries with punitive or unstable trade relationships*

- *Items subject to frequent tariff changes or long customs delays*

- *SKUs with rising landed costs, inconsistent quality, or repeated fulfillment issues*

These are your top candidates for domestic alternatives. Look for U.S.-based or nearshore manufacturers that specialize in smaller production runs or offer flexible terms. Many regional suppliers are actively looking for new business from small and mid-size companies trying to break away from overseas dependency.

Once you find a potential supplier, start with a trial order. Keep the volume small, but use it to test for responsiveness, quality, turnaround time, and flexibility. Don't expect perfect pricing out of the gate—but don't assume it will be prohibitively expensive, either.

Many domestic producers are competitive when you factor in:

- *Lower freight and import costs*

- *Faster delivery timelines*

- *Easier communication and fewer compliance issues*

- *Reduced risk of delays, penalties, or product rework*

- *U.S. legal protections such as the U.C.C. (Uniform Com-*

mercial Code)

Reallocating even 10–20% of your sourcing to domestic vendors can significantly reduce your exposure to overseas volatility. It creates breathing room in your inventory strategy, stabilizes your cash flow, and opens the door to "Made in the U.S.A." branding and marketing opportunities that customers will no doubt increasingly value.

You don't need to cut ties with all foreign suppliers. This is more about building balance into your sourcing strategy so you're not one policy change or shipping delay away from a major crisis.

Diversify Suppliers to Spread Risk

Having only a single supplier for a critical product or component is a huge vulnerability. Even if that supplier is currently reliable, low-cost, and responsive, your entire operation is at risk if circumstances change. Today, global trade volatility can happen overnight.

Recent developments have underscored the importance of diversification. For instance, the United States has imposed 25% tariffs on imports from Canada and Mexico (its strongest and most reliable trade allies), overriding previous trade agreements like the USMCA. These actions have led to retaliatory measures and increased uncertainty in North American trade relations.

To mitigate these types of risks, consider the following strategies:

1. Segment Your Supply Chain by Risk and Value

Not all products carry equal weight. You'll want to prioritize diversification for:

- *High-margin items that drive revenue*

- *Components that are hard to replace quickly*

- *SKUs sourced from countries with unpredictable tariff enforcement or regulatory changes*

2. Consider New Sourcing Regions

Given the current trade tensions in North America, it may be prudent to explore suppliers in regions with more stable trade relations.

Consider areas like:

- ***Southeast Asian*** *countries like Vietnam, Malaysia, and Indonesia*

- ***Eastern European*** *nations such as Poland and the Czech Republic*

- **South American** countries like Colombia and Peru

- **African** countries like Ghana, Nigeria and Kenya

These regions may offer competitive pricing and have established manufacturing sectors that can meet your needs. [1]

3. Build a List of Backup Vendors

You don't need to split volume equally across all suppliers.

Instead try to:

- *Maintain one primary supplier for cost efficiency*

- *Keep one or two secondary vendors ready to activate during peak season, delays, or price shifts*

- *Use small test orders to maintain relationships and assess readiness*

This layered approach gives you leverage when renegotiating with your main supplier and protects you when conditions shift. You also reduce lead time risk, gain pricing intelligence across the market, and avoid the added stress of sourcing from scratch during a crisis.

---

1. See Appendix A, which discusses the topic of emerging markets.

This isn't redundancy for redundancy's sake—it's resilience by design. With a diversified vendor base, you're no longer reacting to problems. You're adapting ahead of them.

Adapt Your Pricing and Messaging Strategy

Rising sourcing costs, tariff volatility, and new supplier relationships all point to one unavoidable reality: your pricing strategy must evolve. But how you update your prices and communicate those changes might mean the difference between customer retention and customer churn.

Small businesses hesitate to raise prices, especially when they fear losing customers to cheaper competitors. But when input costs steadily rise due to tariffs, supply chain constraints, and global uncertainty, holding your prices steady can quickly destroy your profits. What matters most is how you execute the change, not the change itself.

Here's a 4-step process for ensuring that your pricing and messaging accurately reflect reality:

Step 1: Strategically Adjust Pricing

It's important to remember that not every product needs a price increase.

Start by reviewing:

- *SKUs with the highest landed cost increases (especially those sourced from tariff-affected countries)*

- *Items with high turnover and low margins*

- *Products where quality, reliability, or availability have improved due to better suppliers*

Raise prices only where the math demands it. Hold the line where you still have a decent price buffer. Bundle slow-moving items or offer volume discounts to soften the perception of cost increases without sacrificing profit.

Your ultimate goal is not to match your competitor's pricing dollar-for-dollar—it's to ensure your business remains sustainable while delivering consistent value.

Step 2: Communicate Clearly and Confidently

Customers are more likely to accept price changes when they understand why. Vague explanations or silence only breed frustration. Be transparent, but firm.

For example:

> *"Due to ongoing global trade restrictions and increased import costs, we've updated our pricing to en-*

sure product availability and maintain the level of service you expect from us."

Or:

"We've made strategic changes to our supply chain to reduce risk and improve reliability. These changes come with increased cost, but they also allow us to serve you more consistently."

This isn't apologizing—it's owning your business decisions and reinforcing the trust your customers already place in you.

Step 3: Reinforce the Customer Value

If you're charging more for your products, give the customer a solid reason to feel good about it.

Here are some aspects to highlight:

- *Domestic sourcing or shorter lead times*

- *Improved product consistency or reduced backorders*

- *Enhanced service, packaging, or fulfillment reliability*

- *Supporting local jobs or ethical manufacturing*

Price is just one part of the customer experience. Service, transparency, and reliability matter just as much, especially during economic uncertainty.

Step 4: Train and Prepare Your Team

If you have staff, make sure everyone, from sales to customer service, knows how to explain pricing changes with clarity and confidence. Equip them with proper messaging that emphasizes value, reliability, and how you're staying ahead of tariffs or supply chain disruptions.

Your team should never say, *"Sorry, prices went up."*

They should say, *"Here's what we've done to protect (or enhance) your experience, and how that's reflected in our pricing."*

Key Takeaway: Pricing isn't just math—it's communication. Customers don't leave because prices go up. They leave because businesses stop delivering value or go silent when things change.

Focus on Operational Agility

If there's one skill that separates businesses that survive disruption from those that collapse under it, it's agility. Not size. Not funding. Not brand recognition.

Agility.

In a global trade climate where tariffs can spike overnight, shipping lanes get clogged, and trade relations shift with little warning, the ability to move quickly and adapt your operations in real time is a strategic advantage. It's what allows you to stay one step ahead, instead of playing catch-up.

Agility doesn't mean chaos. It means building systems that respond well to change without compromising performance.

Here's how to get started.

Rethink Your Inventory Strategy

Holding too much inventory ties up valuable cash. Holding too little leaves you vulnerable when supply chain delays hit. Your inventory mix might need rebalancing:

- *Increase buffer stock only for your most critical, high-turnover products*

- *Identify which SKUs are most vulnerable to delays from*

countries with volatile trade conditions and prioritize stock there.

- *Consider splitting storage between locations or using a 3PL (third-party logistics) provider that can flex capacity as needed.*

Agile inventory isn't just what you hold—it's about where and how you hold it.

Shorten Your Planning Cycles

When economic turbulence hits, annual planning cycles can quickly become too rigid or outdated. You'll most likely need to plan operations around shorter, reviewable cycles—monthly or quarterly—so you can adjust sourcing, production, and pricing based on real-time data.

Consider the following:

- *Running leaner forecasts that focus on high-probability scenarios*

- *Evaluating supplier performance on a rolling basis, not once per year*

- *Adjusting reorder points based on actual lead time data*

To remain adaptable to emerging market conditions, you'll need the ability to respond faster than they can box you in.

Build Flexibility Into Your Fulfillment Model

If you only have one way to get your product to your customer, you have a single point of failure.

You might want to:

- *Add a backup shipping partner or fulfillment service*

- *Use hybrid shipping strategies (e.g., mix of direct-to-customer and local distribution points)*

- *Stagger order fulfillment windows so you can handle demand spikes without overpromising delivery times*

Small changes in fulfillment workflows can create big improvements in both customer satisfaction and operational control.

Train for Responsiveness

Agility isn't just operational—it's also cultural. If you have a team, build responsiveness into the way they operate and respond:

Normalize the practice of revisiting assumptions every month.

Empower staff to raise red flags early when things seem off.

Treat changing plans as a sign of strength, not weakness.

Resilient businesses don't blindly follow a plan—instead, they're committed to the outcome.

>
> ***Key Takeaway:*** Agility isn't optional. It's how you manage uncertainty without losing quality, trust, or profits. Operational flexibility helps you respond instead of react, which turns disruption into opportunity.

In the next chapter, we'll step back and look at your sourcing strategy as a whole—how to identify domestic manufacturers that meet your needs, and what tools and resources are available to help you find them.

Chapter 5

How to Find Top U.S. Suppliers

N ow that you've audited your supply chain and identified your weak points, the next step is clear: find reliable suppliers closer to home that can meet your needs.

Given the current protectionist trade climate, domestic sourcing is now a competitive necessity for many small businesses. Whether you're looking to avoid punitive tariffs, unreliable foreign logistics, or just gain more control over your lead times, building relationships with manufacturers in the U.S. (or at least outside of high-risk regions) is a smart move.

But this often raises a few concerns:

1. *Where do I even begin looking?*

2. *Can I afford it?*

3. *Will they work with a business my size?*

In this chapter, we'll answer all three questions.

You'll learn where to find suppliers that understand shorter runs, flexible timelines, and limited budgets. We'll discuss ways to make domestic sourcing more accessible, even if you're doing this for the first time. And you'll learn how to vet those suppliers to ensure they're reliable before committing.

Most importantly, you'll see how to phase in domestic sourcing strategically. You don't need to move your entire operation overnight. Just start shifting the parts of your supply chain most exposed to foreign risk.

Start Here: U.S. Databases and Platforms

Finding a domestic manufacturer used to mean endless phone calls, trade shows, and digging through outdated directories. That's no longer the case. Today, powerful tools exist to help small and mid-sized businesses find reliable, qualified suppliers within the U.S. and other trade-stable regions.

Whether you're searching for components, finished products, or custom manufacturing, these platforms can give you a head start. They let you to search by industry, production capability, location, certifications, and minimum order quantity (MOQ). Most importantly, they're designed to work for businesses that aren't necessarily ordering by the truckload.

Here are a handful of sourcing platforms worth investigating:

Thomasnet

https://www.thomasnet.com

Thomasnet is one of the oldest and most comprehensive directories of North American manufacturers. You can search by product type, location, certification (ISO, FDA, etc.), and production capability. Whether you're sourcing sheet metal, electronics, or packaging, Thomasnet connects you directly with the manufacturer—no middlemen.

- Ideal for industrial components, parts, materials, and B2B production

- Many listings include CAD files, downloadable specs, and verified contact info

- Filters available for small-volume manufacturers and custom jobs

Maker's Row

https://www.makersrow.com

Best suited for apparel, accessories, furniture, and consumer goods, Maker's Row connects small brands with U.S.-based manufacturers that accept smaller runs. The platform is intuitive and built with startups in mind.

- Great for fashion, home goods, leather, jewelry, and soft goods

- Offers design and product development services in addition to manufacturing

- Includes messaging features and project management tools

MFG.com

https://www.mfg.com

This platform focuses on custom part manufacturing, especially for metalwork, plastics, machining, and prototyping. You can post your project, receive quotes from vetted manufacturers, and review past job ratings.

- Best for CNC, injection molding, casting, and precision manufacturing

- Especially useful if you're shifting from overseas production and need to prototype, rework or adapt components

- Allows for competitive bidding between suppliers

Kompass

https://us.kompass.com

A global B2B directory that allows you to filter for U.S.-based or regional suppliers. Especially helpful for identifying niche manufacturers or specialized vendors that may not appear in startup-friendly platforms.

- Covers over 60 countries, with strong U.S. representation

- Useful for both sourcing and exporting

- Ideal for businesses planning for future international diversification

Local and State-Level Economic Development Databases

While not a traditional trading platform, many U.S. states and regional economic development agencies provide supplier databases as part of their reshoring and job-creation initiatives. These are often underutilized and free to access.

Examples include directories and resources from states like:

- Ohio — Ohio Economic Development Association (https://ohioeda.com/)

- Texas — Texas Economic Development Corporation (https://businessintexas.com/)

- Georgia — Georgia Economic Developers Association (https://www.geda.org/)

- Michigan — Michigan Economic Development Corporation (https://www.michiganbusiness.org/)

Many states offer supplier matchmaking events, grants, or subsidies for shifting production domestically. Start with your state's Department of Economic Development or Small Business Development Center (SBDC)

Don't be afraid to leverage these resources. Additionally, depending on how global and U.S. trade policy progresses, the Federal Government may also be incentivized to increase visibility and access to domestic resources.

Bonus Tip: If you're just targeting trade-stable partners outside the U.S., consider countries like Vietnam, Poland, or Malaysia (growing manufacturing capacity and less geopolitical friction). These countries are eager to do business with U.S. and can often be accessed through their trade ministries or export promotion agencies.

Vetting Domestic Partners for Reliability

Finding a domestic manufacturer is only the first step. The next (and, arguably more important step), is ensuring they can actually deliver on their promises. Just because a supplier is local doesn't automatically mean they're reliable, cost-effective, or the right fit for your business. You still need to conduct due diligence.

Here's how to vet potential manufacturing partners so you're not just swapping one set of problems for another. The goal is to build relationships with suppliers who will protect your reputation, not put it at risk.

Start with Capabilities, Not Promises

A good supplier knows what they can—and can't—deliver. You'll want specifics:

- *What's their actual production capacity, per day or per shift?*

- *Can they scale up if your demand increases, or will you outgrow them quickly?*

- *What equipment or processes do they use, and how mod-*

ern are their facilities?

- *Do they offer prototyping, small-batch runs, or just high-volume output?*

Ask for documentation such as line sheets, case studies, and sample production schedules. Vague answers simply won't cut it.

Look For Quality Systems and Certifications

Even for small orders, quality matters. If a domestic manufacturer isn't meeting basic standards, you'll pay for it in returns, rework, and lost trust.

You'll want to look for:

- *ISO 9001 or industry-specific certifications (FDA, GMP, UL, etc.)*

- *In-house quality control processes: what checks happen, and when?*

- *Historical defect rates and how customer complaints are handled (timing and satisfaction metrics)*

Don't guess. Request a sample product (or lot) to assess quality firsthand.

Ask the Right Questions Up Front

It's important to remember that you're not just interviewing a supplier—they're auditioning to become a core part of your business. It's time to *'get down to brass tacks.'*

Ask questions such as:

- *What's your average lead time?*

- *How do you handle supply shortages or order changes?*

- *What's your MOQ (minimum order quantity)?*

- *What are your payment terms and penalties, if any?*

- *Have you worked with companies in my industry and/or with similar volume needs?*

Don't just take their word—verify. Ask for 2–3 references, preferably small business clients with similar needs. If they can't—or won't—provide any, that's a sign that you might want to move on.

Conduct a Site Visit or Virtual Tour of the Facility

If possible, visit the facility yourself. If that's not feasible, ask for a virtual tour or a video walkthrough of the production floor.

You'll learn more from a 5-minute video of their workflow than from a polished sales deck.

What to look for:

- *Cleanliness, organization, and safety protocols*

- *Workflow efficiency*

- *Signs of understaffing, clutter, or outdated equipment*

You're not looking for perfection here. You're seeing for yourself whether the operation can support consistency and scale without falling apart under pressure.

Start Small, Then Scale Up

Once you've identified a potential partner, start small. Place a test order.

Observe closely how they handle:

- *Communication during production*

- *Adherence to timelines*

- *Accuracy and quality of the finished product*

- *Packaging and delivery consistency*

A trial run gives you leverage and clarity. If they perform well, you can ramp up with confidence. If not, you've minimized the risk and cost of failure.

Key Takeaway: Domestic sourcing can give you speed, stability, and quality—but only if you work with the right partners. Vetting upfront saves you time, money, and possible reputation damage later.

Negotiate Better Terms Without Volume Guarantees

Another common misconception among small business owners is that unless you place massive orders, you have absolutely no leverage with a domestic manufacturer.

That's simply not true.

What you may lack in volume, you can often make up for in flexibility, reliability, and long-term potential. And in unstable trade climates, even suppliers are trying to reduce their dependence on large, unpredictable clients. Therefore, small, consistent orders can be more attractive than you think.

But to get favorable terms, you need to know what to ask for—and how to frame it.

Understand What the Supplier Actually Wants

Your supplier wants more than just a big check.

They're also looking for:

- **Predictability:** *Orders they can plan around*

- **Consistency:** *Fewer change orders or last-minute adjustments*

- **Low-friction relationships:** *Clients who pay on time, communicate clearly, and don't micromanage the process*

- **Upside:** *A customer who might grow into a larger account*

If you can offer any (or all) of these—even without massive order volumes—you have a powerful negotiating point.

Offer Something Valuable Beyond Money

Even if you can't commit to, say, 10,000 units a month, you might be able to offer valuable *quid pro quo* that identifies you as a top-tier client.

Here are some examples:

- ***Rolling forecasts*** *of demand to help them plan production cycles*

- ***Extended partnership terms****, like a 6- or 12-month working agreements*

- ***Low-maintenance communication****, such as batching updates or submitting purchase orders in a consistent format*

- ***Continuous referrals or marketing****, especially if you're a well-known brand in a niche market, or have extensive contacts in your industry*

The key is to focus on becoming the easiest client your supplier has to work with—not the biggest.

Prioritize Flexibility Over Price

If you simply go into a negotiation *"head-first,"* trying to instantly shave 15% off the unit cost, you'll more than likely encounter resistance. But remember that price is not the only concession that matters when negotiating with experienced suppliers.

You might also want to gauge flexibility on:

- *Better lead times*

- *Reduced minimum order quantities (MOQs)*

- *Better payment terms (e.g., 50% up front, 50% on delivery)*

- *Bundled services like packaging or fulfillment*

Asking for these types of concessions will more likely result in a *"yes"* from the supplier. These requests may seem minor, but they often matter more to your bottom-line cash flow than a slight cost reduction.

Use Trial Runs as an Entry Point

If you've completed a successful test order, you've already earned a better conversation with your supplier, whether you realize it or not. Use that as a starting point, or even leverage for future negotiations.

Here's an example:

> *"We liked the quality and communication on the first run. But, if we can tighten up lead time and move to 30-day payment terms, we'd be ready to place more frequent orders."*

This kind of incremental, logic-based negotiation is more effective than bluffing or overpromising.

Put Everything in Writing

Even if the initial order volume is small, take the extra time to retain a lawyer and have her draft a basic supply agreement that outlines (at minimum):

- *Price per unit*

- *Payment terms*

- *Lead times*

- *Revision or cancellation policy*

- *Terms for quality disputes or rejected goods*

If you are handed an agreement by a supplier, always have a legal professional review and explain the agreement, especially any terms that may be unfamiliar or seem vague. Having your paperwork in order makes you look professional, and sets a clear foundation if things happen to go sideways later.

Include Financial Diligence When Negotiating

When you're working with a new manufacturer (especially a small one), you're well within your rights to ask about stability before negotiating deeper terms. A supplier who's on shaky financial ground might agree to overly-generous terms they know they can't fulfill.

Red flags might include:

- *Reluctance to discuss capacity*

- *Dodging questions about staffing, equipment, or financing*

- *Multiple recent UCC liens, lawsuits or unfavorable news reports*

Good negotiation protects both sides. It sets expectations early and avoids confusion down the line when delays or shortages can cost you real money.

Key Takeaway: You don't need massive volume to negotiate. You need predictability, professionalism, and a value-based approach. When you speak the vendor's language and are easy to work with, you earn better terms.

Build Long-Term Relationships with Suppliers

Finding a reliable supplier is only half of the equation. The other half is retaining them.

Once you've established a relationship with a trustworthy vendor, your goal should shift from *"placing orders"* to *"building partnerships."* Long-term supplier relationships reduce your operational friction, improve your negotiating power, and increase your ability to pivot in volatile markets. The better your partnership, the more likely they'll go the extra mile when it matters. Here's how to build that kind of relationship (especially if you're a small business without massive volumes.

Be Clear and Consistent in All Communication

Your supplier isn't a mind reader. And they shouldn't have to guess what you want. Communicate future needs, current updates, and order changes as early as possible. The smoother you are to work with, the more reliable your service will become.

Be sure to:

- *Send POs and order adjustments in writing*

- *Confirm delivery timelines early*

- *Give a "heads-up" if demand is expected to spike or dip*

- *Send questions in "batches," rather than constantly "drip-feeding" them*

Remember: professionalism sets the tone for the relationship.

Pay on Time. Every Time.

Do you still want the *"red carpet"* treatment when lead times get tight? Start by becoming the client who *always* pays on time.

Seriously.

Suppliers prioritize clients who respect payment terms and don't play games with invoices. Even if your order is smaller, reliable cash flow makes you more valuable than a large but unpredictable customer.

If you're ever going to miss a payment deadline, let them know early and offer a plan.

When it comes to money, silence . . . kills trust.

Stay in Touch During Quiet Periods

Don't disappear when things are slow. A quick check-in, a thank-you email, or sharing how your product performed in the market shows that *you're invested in the relationship—not just the next transaction*.

Suppliers remember clients who stay engaged year-round, not just during peak times, or when a problem arises.

Don't Just Transact. Collaborate.

When a supplier understands your long-term goals, they can help you reach them. Ask for input.

For example:

- *Share growth targets[1] so they can prepare for increased production capacity*

- *Get their input on cost-saving alternatives or material improvements*

- *Involve them in new product development early—they may suggest better production methods or catch issues before they cost you time and money.*

The best suppliers aren't just vendors. They're problem-solvers. But they can only help if you give them insight into your pain points and growth aspirations.

Handle Issues Promptly and Professionally

Mistakes will happen eventually. A shipment might be delayed. A spec might be missed. What matters most is how you respond to the problem.

Instead of quickly jumping to blame the other party:

- *Document the issue clearly*

- *Ask for their perspective*

- *Work together on a solution*

- *Evaluate whether it's a one-time problem or a pattern*

Long-term relationships survive hiccups when both parties stay solution-focused instead of blame-oriented.

Give Public Praise (and Private Feedback)

If your supplier is doing a great job, tell them. Better yet—tell others.

- *Leave a positive review on sourcing platforms*

- *Refer them to other businesses in your network*

- *Allow them to list you as a customer reference when pursuing new clients*

This turns you into more than just a buyer. You're a valuable ally in their long-term growth.

>  ***Key Takeaway:*** The more you act like a partner, the more you'll be treated like one. Strong supplier relationships provide more flexibility, faster service, and better terms without having to beg for them.

In the next chapter, we'll drill down a bit more and explore how to adjust your product line to reduce or avoid challenges caused by tariffs and global trade tensions.

Chapter 6
How to Pivot Your Product Line

S upply chain changes only work if your overall product strategy supports them. It doesn't matter how fast or efficiently you can source materials if you're still selling products that are too expensive to make, too slow to deliver, or too vulnerable to disruption.

In this chapter, we'll take a hard look at whether your product line makes sense, and how to make sure it matches your sourcing capabilities. Adapting your product strategy doesn't mean abandoning your catalog or reinventing your business.

It means taking a step back and asking the right questions:

- *Which products are costing you more than they're worth?*

- *Which SKUs come from volatile regions, and which can be redesigned or simplified?*

- *Can you swap overseas components for domestic alternatives, without sacrificing your margins?*

- *Are you offering products that allow room to breathe, or does complexity box you in?*

This is where smart businesses find their advantage—not by competing on volume or price, but by building lean, resilient product lines that can survive disruptions and still deliver value to their customers.

Let's begin with the *"low-hanging fruit"*: identifying which products are doing more harm than good.

What to Stop Selling Now

Sometimes, the most brilliant business move you can make is to stop selling something.

When tariffs are climbing, lead times are slipping, and costs are chewing through your margins, it's not enough to change suppliers—you also need to assess whether your current product mix is still worth it, given your sourcing strategy. Some products simply cost more to carry than they deliver in profit, flexibility, or customer retention.

Your job isn't just to sell stuff—it's to sell stuff *in a smart and profitable way.* Focus your energy on the right products for the right people, at the right time.

Here's how to determine what should come off your shelves, at least for now.

Products From High-Tariff Regions

Start with anything still tied to countries with high punitive tariff rates, unpredictable customs enforcement, or logistical slowdowns. If a product's key components come from a region where costs are rising and shipping is unstable, it's likely under-performing—whether you realize it or not.

Take a step back and ask:

- *Have my landed costs for this product increased by more than 15% in the last year?*

- *Are shipping delays hurting my delivery promises or re-stocking timelines?*

- *Is this item constantly forcing me into backorders, re-funds, or causing customer complaints?*

If the answer is yes, consider phasing it out, reworking it with local inputs, or limiting it to pre-orders (or special runs).

Low-Margin, High-Volume SKUs

These products might keep cash flowing, but they also drain your time and working capital. If you're moving large volumes but only netting pennies per sale—and absorbing all the risk—you're putting in too much for too little.

You'll want to cut or restructure:

- *Products that need frequent restocking but have minimal or fragile profit margins*

- *SKUs that force you into high MOQs with suppliers, tying up cash in inventory*

- *Items where a slight increase in cost (tariff, freight, material) wipes out your entire profit margin*

You're not in business to stay busy. You're in business to make money.

Complex Assembly / Imported Subcomponents

You're unnecessarily multiplying your risk if a product needs multiple parts from multiple countries. Each component is another opportunity for cost volatility, shipment delays, or customs issues.

Ask yourself:

- *Can this product be simplified?*

- *Can I offer a pared-down version that's easier to produce locally?*

- *Would dropping this product free up space for something more strategic or profitable?*

If the complexity outweighs the benefit, it's time to reconsider.

'Dogs' That Drain Space and Capital

If you're still holding items that haven't moved in 90+ days and show no signs of revival, don't wait for the perfect buyer—reclaim that capital now.

Slow movers (i.e., *'dogs'*) might be tied to old sourcing models, outdated customer demand, or pricing strategies that no longer make sense.

Get rid of them quickly through:

- *Bundles or clearance events*

- *Converting them into giveaway or incentive items*

- *Licensing the product to another business with better margins, better brand alignment or broader market reach*

What truly matters is making space for product lines that are aligned with your new strategy, not burdened by legacy inventory.

Products That Create More Problems Than Loyalty

If a product causes an excessive amount of returns, complaints, or support tickets, take a closer look. In today's environment, *reputation loss* is more expensive than *product loss*.

Ask:

- *Am I losing customers because of shipping, quality, delays, or pricing?*

- *Can those issues be traced back to sourcing or fulfillment?*

- *Is this product actually building brand loyalty—or quietly eroding it?*

If a product is hurting your customer trust or straining your team's capacity, it's probably not worth keeping around.

Key Takeaway: If a product doesn't serve your margins, customer, or supply chain, it doesn't belong in your lineup. Cutting SKUs doesn't always mean shrinking your business—it means sharpening it.

Products You'll Want to Prioritize

While some products simply won't cut it under the weight of tariffs and sourcing disruptions, others will naturally hold up regardless of global instability. These products are generally simple to produce, faster to deliver, easier to localize, and less dependent on international supply chains.

It's important to find these *'winners'* in your product lineup or start producing them.

Here's what you'll want to prioritize going forward:

Domestic Products With Competitive Costs

Not everything can be affordably made in the U.S., but plenty of things can.

Especially things like:

- *Apparel basics (tees, hoodies, socks)*

- *Packaging supplies (boxes, sleeves, inserts)*

- *Custom prints, personalized or niche-specific products*

- *Leather accessories, candles, and other handcrafted goods*

- *Metal or plastic parts that require simple molds or ma-*

chining processes

Building a product line around items like these reduces reliance on foreign ports, customs, and geopolitical risk. You also build turnaround speed into your business, which creates trust.

Items Without Multi-Step Assembly or Fragile Supply Chains

The more moving parts you have in your product(s), the more exposure you have.

Instead, look for:

- *Single-material items (e.g., molded silicone, glassware, wood products)*

- *Products made with regionally abundant inputs (e.g., U.S.-grown cotton, recycled paper)*

- *Designs that allow for modular substitution if a component becomes unavailable*

Remember that every unnecessary component removed is one less opportunity for delays, shortages, or damage to your reputation.

Digital / Semi-Digital Products That Reduce Inventory

While not every business can take their products digital, hybrid models do exist.

Consider the following options:

- *Products that include a downloadable guide, app, or high-value add-on*

- *Subscription-based products where physical fulfillment can be batched or delayed without damaging customer experience*

- *Kits or bundles that include a high-margin digital element (courses, instructions, digital apps or tools)*

These are margin boosters that can potentially lower your dependency on freight, customs, and warehouse space.

Locally or Regionally Sourced SKUs

Products that can be directly tied to your local city, state, or neighborhood not only build brand loyalty, but they're often easier to source and fulfill.

Look for:

- *Regionally produced materials or artisan collaborations*

- *Products that highlight "Made in [Your City / County / State]" as part of the brand story*

- *Short-run seasonal items that reflect local pride or popular local demand*

The closer you are to your sources, the faster you can pivot, adapt, and restock your product line without relying on cargo shipping timelines.

Replenishable Items with Steady Demand and Local Fulfillment

Think consumables, refills, and household goods—products that don't go out of style and don't require globally-sourced components.

Some examples might include:

- *Soap, skincare, or wellness items using U.S.-based (or even locally sourced) ingredients — think local farms, co-ops, farmers markets, etc.*

- *Office products with minimal complexity*

- *Repeat-purchase hobby products or crafting items*

If you get these items domestically and keep reorder friction low, they can quickly turn into revenue anchors.

Key Takeaway: Resilient products aren't necessarily the flashiest, but they offer control over lead times, quality, and pricing. In a high-risk environment, control keeps you profitable while competitors scramble.

Redesign or Simplify Existing Products

You don't always have to totally scrap an existing product to insulate it from logistical challenges—sometimes, simply reconfiguring it or stripping away the parts that make it vulnerable is just as effective.

Unfortunately, though, tariffs, logistics delays, and materials shortages often expose a hard truth:

Most products are far more complex than they need to be.

For instance, a popular design that relies on four vendors across three countries is a liability, not a strength. The goal should be to preserve the core of what makes your product valuable while removing what slows it down, drives up cost, or creates operational chaos.

This is where simplification becomes a competitive strategy.

Here are some ideas you might want to consider:

1. Identify What's Non-Negotiable

Start by breaking your product(s) down.

Ask yourself:

- *What do my customers actually care about?*

- *What features, materials, or finishes are absolutely essential to my product's value and function?*

- *What parts are mostly aesthetic or marketing-driven, and can be easily substituted without killing sales?*

If your customer only notices or cares about the end result, don't over-engineer the process behind it. Focus on protecting what they experience and value, not what's *"behind the curtain."*

2. Eliminate or Substitute Imported Components

If your product line relies on parts from countries with punitive tariffs or frequent customs delays, it's time to start looking for substitutions.

Explore the possibility of sourcing similar components from domestic or nearshore suppliers. Another option might be to find raw materials that are regionally abundant, even if this means using recycled or repurposed products. Perhaps the product in question could also be redesigned to reduce dependency on more complex sub-assemblies.

Sometimes, the difference between a risky product and a stable one requires updating just one part of the bill of materials.

3. Streamline Packaging and Presentation

Custom inserts, specialty boxes, and imported packaging materials might have looked great in 2017, but now they might be compromising your supply chain.

Explore how you can redesign your packaging to:

- *Use U.S.-based printers and die-cutters*

- *Fit standard box sizes to reduce shipping costs and delays*

- *Reduce inventory that requires special handling, temperature control, or lengthy lead times*

Your packaging shouldn't be the most expensive or fragile. Nor should it cause unnecessary delays within your business model.

4. Standardize Whenever Possible

Likewise, take a hard look at any aspects of your manufacturing process that require a custom assembly process. This can cause bottlenecks in your operation.

Ask yourself:

- *Can you consolidate SKUs by color, size, or variant?*

- *Can multiple products share the same component or packaging?*

- *Can your assembly process be done with fewer steps or with less training?*

The more standardization you build into the process, the faster you can fulfill orders, train staff, and onboard new vendors if needed.

5. Use Customer Feedback to Prioritize Changes

If you're not sure which changes are safe to make, look to your customers. Use customer-driven data such as product reviews, return data, and support tickets to spot the areas where:

- *Quality isn't meeting expectations*

- *Features are underused (or unwanted)*

- *Frustration is tied to size, weight, complexity, or usability*

You might be shocked to find that the parts you're most worried about removing ... aren't even being noticed or valued by your customers.

Key Takeaway: This isn't about cheapening products—it's more about *"bulletproofing"* them. A simpler product isn't just easier to make. It's easier to scale, ship, explain, price, and sell.

Low-Risk Expansion Strategies

Expanding your product line doesn't always mean large investments in tooling, equipment, hiring additional staff, or importing more raw materials. The smarter path may be the *safer* one—adding products or services without increasing your exposure to sourcing volatility or operational complexity.

Low-risk expansion models allow you to grow strategically by using what you already have, tapping into existing infrastructure, or partnering with others who can absorb some of the risk.

Here are some strategies:

White Labeling

White labeling lets you sell a pre-manufactured product under your own brand. It's a great solution when you're looking to expand into a new category quickly. Or, perhaps you don't have the capacity or staff to manage manufacturing; and the product is standard enough not to require extensive customization.

Look for U.S.-based white label providers in industries like:

- *Skincare and cosmetics*

- *Supplements and wellness*

- *Coffee, tea, and packaged foods*

- *Office supplies and lifestyle goods*

Some unique benefits include:

- *No need to manage on-site production*

- *Speed to market*

- *Lower upfront investment*

If you decide to go this route, you'll want to watch for high MOQ requirements, packaging limitations, and exclusivity clauses.

Licensing an Existing Product

Licensing allows you to sell or co-brand a product someone else owns, generally for a percentage of sales or a flat fee. This allows you to benefit from a proven product (or quickly test out a new market) without starting from scratch.

This may work especially well when:

- *You want to test a new category without building internal expertise*

- *You've identified a strong brand or supplier looking to expand their reach into a new domain*

- *You want to localize an existing product for your market or niche area*

Pay close attention to: traditionally underserved, niche, or little-known regional producers, smaller-scale inventors, or even trade partners in complementary industries with overlap into your domain of expertise.

U.S.-Based Dropshipping

Dropshipping isn't new, but as technology has steadily improved, the model has evolved. Today, you can quickly and easily partner up with U.S.-based dropshipping providers who:

- *Offer faster shipping than overseas alternatives*

- *Specialize in niche product categories*

- *Allow you to focus on branding, sales, and customer experience instead of product development*

Domestic dropshipping is especially useful when:

- *You want to test out demand without stocking physical inventory*

- *You're not quite ready to invest in packaging or fulfillment*

- *You want to supplement your core product with accessories, seasonal offers or add-on products*

Here's a pro-tip: Choose dropshipping partners that integrate netaly with your order system and offer a completely white-label brand experience, including receipts, packing slips, and packaging.

Print-on-Demand (POD)

POD platforms let you sell custom designs on products like apparel, mugs, notebooks, or packaging inserts—without keeping physical inventory.

This is best for:

- *Testing new branding or creative angles*

- *Seasonal or promotional items or limited-time runs*

- *Expanding into low-risk merch for loyal customers*

A handful of popular U.S.-based POD providers include: Printful, Printify, Gooten, and Apliiq (for fashion).

Bundling or Curating Products

Sometimes, the most effective way to expand is to repurpose. You can quickly create new SKUs by:

- *Bundling multiple products together*

- *Offering limited-edition kits or seasonal sets*

- *Curating new products from domestic partners (i.e., using some of the techniques listed above) to create a unique branded experience*

Here's why it works:

- *No new production required*

- *Higher perceived customer value*

- *Helps move inventory while introducing "new" products*

> **Key Takeaway:** Expansion doesn't have to add risk. These strategies let you test new markets, serve new customers, and diversify revenue while keeping your overhead low.

Communicate Changes Without Losing Trust

Before closing out this chapter, I'd like to share some practical suggestions for how to communicate to customers when you need to make changes to your product line, SKUs, or processes.

It's important to remember that raising prices, changing suppliers, or discontinuing products doesn't just affect your operations—it also affects your customers' experience. And in a world where brand loyalty is fragile and expectations are high, *how you communicate* changes matters just as much as *what you change*.

The good news?

Most customers aren't opposed to change. They just want to be kept in the loop, and, more importantly, they want to understand the story behind the change. The brands that maintain customer trust through disruption are the ones that communicate clearly, honestly, and early—*before* their customers start asking difficult questions.

So, here are some ways to communicate changes without losing customer confidence or brand equity:

Lead With Why, Not Just What

Don't just announce that a product is going away or that prices are going up. Start with the reason. When you give people context, they're more likely to understand, and even support your decision.

For example:

> *"To continue offering reliable service in the face of rising supplier costs, we've made the decision to update our pricing structure starting next month."*

Or:

> *"Due to global shipping delays and increased raw material costs, we're discontinuing [Product Name] and shifting focus to items we can deliver consistently without compromise."*

This approach isn't damage control. It's transparency.

Use a Confident, Professional Tone

When communicating with customers, avoid sounding defensive or apologetic. You're not making excuses, you're making smart business decisions that prioritize customer experience, product quality, and long-term sustainability.

Instead of saying . . .

"We hate to do this, but..."

"Unfortunately, we have no choice..."

Say . . .

"This is part of our strategy to serve you better"

"We're making this change to protect quality, consistency, and delivery times."

Confidence builds trust. Wavering erodes it.

Reinforce the Value You Provide

Every change should tie back to the value you (or your product) provide to the customer or end-user. If you're raising prices, explain to customers what they're getting in return. If you're switching to domestic suppliers, don't forget to highlight the benefits, such as:

- *Faster delivery*

- *Higher quality materials*

- *Lower environmental impact*

- *Supporting U.S. jobs or local makers*

You'll want to actively convey the message that you're not just increasing prices arbitrarily—you're upgrading their overall experience.

Use Cross-Channel Communication

When communicating changes (especially sensitive ones) use every platform your customers touch:

- *Email newsletters (with a human, direct tone)*

- *A banner or announcement bar on your website*

- *Product pages with clear "updated pricing" or "domestic-sourced" callouts*

- *FAQs that explain changes in detail*

- *Social media posts to reinforce the message and address questions*

The more consistent (and persistent) your messaging, the more comfortable and confident your customers will feel.

Turn Changes Into 'Brand Moments'

If you're making positive shifts like moving to domestic suppliers, or upgrading packaging—treat it like a win, and an opportunity to spotlight your brand. Document the journey. Show behind-the-scenes photos. Celebrate the decision publicly.

For example:

> *"We're proud to announce that starting this fall, 100% of our shipping materials will be made in the U.S. drastically cutting lead times and waste, without raising prices."*

Changes handled proactively can strengthen brand loyalty.

Prepare for Pushback (and Respond Intelligently)

Some customers will ask tough questions. Others may vent. The key is to stay professional and firm on your stance:

- *Reaffirm the reason for the change*

- *Focus on what's improving*

- *Offer options if available (e.g., last chance to buy before pricing increases hit)*

If necessary, use a short response script for customer service staff so every reply is consistent and respectful.

Here are some examples:

Sample Email Response: Price Increase

Subject: Re: Pricing Update

Hi [Customer Name],

Thanks for reaching out and for being a loyal part of the [Your Brand Name] community.

We understand that price increases are never ideal, and we want to be transparent about why this change is happening.

Over the past year, the cost of materials, packaging, and shipping has risen sharply—especially for products sourced from countries with high tariffs and unpredictable logistics. Rather than cutting corners or compromising on quality, we made the decision to shift toward more reliable domestic suppliers. This helps us deliver faster, with greater consistency, and with less risk of being out of stock or experiencing excessive shipping delays.

The new pricing reflects our investment in quality and stability. We're confident the value you receive will continue to exceed your expectations.

If you have questions or concerns, we're here to talk through them. And if you'd like help finding alternatives within your budget, we're happy to recommend some options.

We appreciate your continued support and understanding as we grow (and adapt) with you.

Warm regards

Sample Customer Service Script
(Live Chat / Phone / Social Response)

Customer: *"Why are your prices higher now? I used to pay less for this exact same product."*

Response: *Great question—I hear you. We recently made the decision to update our pricing to reflect rising costs in materials and international logistics. Instead of compromising on quality or making our products less reliable, we chose to work with domestic suppliers. This helps us ship faster and stay consistent in uncertain conditions.*

We're always mindful of pricing, and we've only made adjustments where absolutely necessary. If there's a specific concern or if you'd like help finding an alternative, I'm more than happy to help.

Sample Email Response: Product Discontinuation

Hi [Customer Name],

Thank you for your message—and for your past support of our [Product Name].

We know this product was a favorite for many, and deciding to discontinue it wasn't easy. Due to rising costs, supply chain instability, and extended lead times, we could no longer guarantee the consistent quality and availability that our customers expect.

Rather than continue offering a product we couldn't fully stand behind, we've chosen instead to focus on items we can deliver reliably, quickly, and at the level of quality you deserve.

That said, we're currently exploring new alternatives and would love to keep you updated if we bring something similar back in the future. In the meantime, I'd be happy to recommend comparable products that are still in stock and ready to ship.

We genuinely appreciate your loyalty and understanding.

Warm regards

Sample Email Response: Extended Shipping Delays

Subject: Re: Shipping Delay Update

Hi [Customer Name],

Thank you for reaching out—and I understand your frustration.

Global shipping and customs delays have impacted many of our suppliers, especially for products sourced from areas facing increased tariffs and regulatory hold-ups. While we've made major improvements to our sourcing strategy—including shifting to more domestic production—some backorders and delays are still occurring as we transition.

I can assure you that your order is still on the way, and we're monitoring it closely. We're also actively working to shorten our supply chain to prevent issues like this in the future.

We know waiting isn't ideal, and we truly appreciate your patience. If you'd prefer a refund or would like help selecting an in-stock alternative, just let us know—we're happy to help either way.

Thanks again for sticking with us.

Best,

[Your Name]

Sample Quick Response Scripts
(Live Chat / Phone / Social Response)

Product Discontinuation:

"I totally understand why you're disappointed—we had a lot of love for that product too. Unfortunately, due to ongoing sourcing and quality issues, we had to

discontinue it. We'd rather pause than deliver some-
thing inconsistent. I'd be happy to recommend a com-
parable alternative that's available now if you'd like."

Shipping Delay:

"We're really sorry for the delay. Some of our ship-
ments are still affected by port congestion and customs
processing in high-tariff regions. That said, we're ac-
tively transitioning to faster, more reliable suppliers,
and delays like this should be less frequent going for-
ward. Let me check your order status now and see what
I can do to help."

> *Key Takeaway:* Customers don't expect
> perfection. They just want to know that the
> decisions you make are thoughtful, fair, and
> show respect for their pain points. Commu-
> nicate with clarity and confidence.

In the next chapter, we'll talk about how to build the mindset,
infrastructure, and flexibility to adapt (not just react) when
global trade conditions start to become turbulent.

Chapter 7

How to Weather Stormy Trade Climates

You can't control international trade policy. You can't stop port congestion, prevent geopolitical tension, or stabilize global fuel prices. But you can control how your business responds when those things happen.

And they will.

In this chapter, we'll focus on how to anticipate and prepare for disruption.

We're entering an era where trade disruptions are no longer isolated events. They're recurring themes of global commerce in a closely intertwined world. As we've seen in the early months of 2025, tariffs can be imposed with little warning. Export restrictions, container shortages, and shipping cost spikes are also becoming standard. Adapting to this new reality means that the only way to stay competitive is to plan your operations so that they don't collapse under pressure.

Resilience doesn't mean having all the answers. It means staying ready when the questions change.

Let's begin with the first critical skill: spotting disruption on the horizon before it hits your bottom line.

Spotting Global Disruptions Early

By the time most businesses react to a trade disruption, it's already too late. They're chasing containers stuck at the port, scrambling to find new suppliers, or explaining delays to angry customers.

Your unique advantage as a small business isn't in forecasting the future—it's noticing the *"tremors"* before the *"big quake"* hits. The earlier you identify a shift in global trade or supply stability, the more options you have to respond without panic or profit loss.

Here's how to stay alert, informed, and prepared—without spending hours reading policy briefs.

Watch Trade Policy Announcements Closely

Most major tariffs that impact businesses don't just pop up out of nowhere. Most often, they're preceded by official government statements, industry lobbying, leaked drafts of trade proposals and early news reports from economic summits or bilateral talks.

To stay ahead of news, try setting up Google Alerts for terms like:

- *"USTR announcement" (Office of the U.S. Trade Representative)*

- *"tariff increase"*

- *"WTO ruling"*

- *"trade negotiations [your country] [key suppliers' countries]"*

Alternatively, bookmark official sources like:

- Office of the United States Trade Representative (ustr.gov)

- World Trade Organization (wto.org)

- U.S. Customs and Border Protection (cbp.gov)

These sites generally post updates before the ripple effects hit mainstream news outlets.

Monitor Commodity Prices and Global Shipping Trends

Disruptions also may show up in raw material and freight data before they hit your suppliers.

Watch closely for:

- *Spikes in steel, aluminum, oil, or key input prices*

- *Sudden increases in global shipping container rates*

- *Freight index volatility (e.g., Drewry World Container Index or Baltic Dry Index)*

You don't need to track every metric—just the ones that directly affect your core products. For instance, if packaging is critical to your business, monitor paper and corrugate trends. If you sell metal goods, watch aluminum and copper prices.

When those numbers shift quickly, it's often the first sign of a supply chain pinch.

Examples of data from the **Drewy World Container Index (WCI)**:

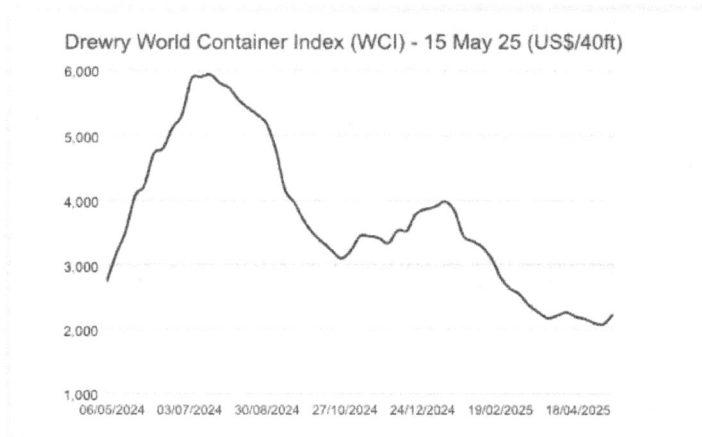

Drewry World Container Index (WCI) - 15 May 25 (US$/40ft)

Drewry WCI: Trade Routes from Shanghai (US$/40ft)

Pay Attention to Geopolitical Flashpoints

Global trade doesn't just follow business and economics—it follows politics even more closely.

Be on the lookout for:

- *Border closures or military escalations*

- *Political instability in key supplier nations*

- *Sanctions, export restrictions, or new import inspections*

- *Sudden changes in diplomatic relationships (e.g., withdrawal from trade agreements)*

Even if your product isn't directly affected, a disruption in one part of the world can cascade through shipping lanes, production schedules, and customs prioritization.

Follow Trade Journals and Associations

Every industry has a handful of specialized sources that report on supply chain news earlier and in more detail than general media.

Some examples include:

- ***Food & Beverage:*** *Food Logistics (foodlogistics.com), The Packer (thepacker.com)*

- ***Apparel & Textiles:*** *Sourcing Journal (sourcingjourn al.com), Just Style (just-style.com)*

- ***Consumer Goods & Retail:*** *Supply Chain Dive (sup plychaindive.com), RetailWire (retailwire.com)*

- ***Manufacturing:*** *IndustryWeek (industryweek.com) , Modern Materials Handling (mmh.com)*

These sources often contain interviews with key industry players: customs brokers, port authorities, and logistics providers that offer real-time insight, not just retrospective analysis.

Here's an example from Sourcing Journal magazine:

CAN SUSTAINABILITY SURVIVE THESE TUMULTUOUS
TIMES?
READ THE SUSTAINABILITY REPORT

SOURCING
JOURNAL

LOG IN   SUBSCRIBE

DENIM   FOOTWEAR   SUSTAINABILITY   WEBINARS   REPORTS   LOGISTICS   VIDEO   SUSTAINABILITY SUMMIT

LOGISTICS
Tariff Tracker

MATERIALS
Material World

TECHNOLOGY
Byte-Sized AI

SNAPSHOT

1 Target Challenged by Tariffs,
   Weak Q1 Sales and Profit Miss

2 Shares of VF Corp. Sink After Q4
   Revenue Miss

3 Google Enriches Shopping
   Features With AI Upgrades

4 Walmart Says It Will Increase
   Prices on Some Goods Because
   of Tariffs

5 Temu Re-Ups Direct-from-China
   Shipments Amidst Tariff Pause

Bangladesh, US Engage in Free Trade Agreement Talks

A deal could greatly bolster the country's ready-made garment sector, which accounts for the bulk of its...

BY KATE NISHIMURA

ADVERTISEMENT

CentricSoftware
Speed Time to Market

If something is affecting your business, chances are that it is also affecting businesses around the world. You can often gain a treasure trove of information simply by signing up for free newsletters.

Build a Simple Internal Alert System

You don't need a full research team on retainer. Just set up a few basic tools:

Google Alerts for your product categories + key countries

Weekly check-ins on 2–3 data sources relevant to your sector

A free email subscriptions to your industry's top trade newsletters

A standing 15-minute weekly review of headlines and freight indicators

You certainly don't need to obsess over every headline. Building an *"early-warning radar"* that helps you shift from reacting to planning is just as effective.

Key Takeaway: The faster you see the change, the more choices you have. Early movers quickly adapt sourcing, cash flow, and messaging. Late movers are forced to explain what went wrong.

The Three Pillars of Resilience: Inventory, Cash and Labor

Trade disruptions are unpredictable. but, your ability to withstand them isn't.

Building resilience isn't sitting around waiting for a crisis to happen—it's structuring your operations to absorb shocks without collapsing. When ports shut down, tariffs spike, or suppliers vanish, it's the businesses with a buffer (not the ones with the biggest budget) that survive.

Resilience starts with three core pillars: inventory, cash, and labor.

Inventory: Create a Buffer. Don't Blindly Stockpile.

You don't need a warehouse full of product to be prepared. You just need the right product, in the right place, with just enough margin to buy yourself time during a disruption.

Here's how to do it:

- **Create safety stock** *for your top 10–20% revenue-generating products, especially those with overseas exposure or long lead times*

- **Diversify warehouse locations** *or use a 3PL (third-party logistics provider) with regional fulfillment centers to reduce geographic bottlenecks*

- **Use ABC inventory analysis** *to prioritize your stock based on value and velocity, not emotion or sentimentality (see appendix).*

- **Set reorder points based on actual lead time**, *not supplier promises*

If you're only re-ordering when you run out, you're not lean—you're fragile.

Cash: Preserve Liquidity Before You Need It

During a disruption, cash is leverage. It gives you flexibility to pivot suppliers, expedite shipping, or ride out a sudden dip in sales.

Here are some ideas to stay *'cash ready'*:

- ***Strengthen your cash position*** *by regularly reviewing your burn rate and reducing nonessential spend, especially during a recession*

- ***Negotiate payment terms*** *with suppliers so you're not front-loading costs (e.g., 50/50 split, net-30 or net-60 terms)*

- ***Secure a line of credit*** *before you need it—banks are more generous when you're not in a bind*

- ***Forecast cash flow monthly****, not quarterly, especially during volatile periods*

Profit matters. Cash flow is survival.

Labor: Cross-Train, Simplify, and Stay Flexible

When disruptions hit, you don't just lose products. You also lose people. Illness, turnover, burnout, or even local disasters can shrink your labor capacity overnight.

Here's how to stay flexibile:

- ***Cross-train employees*** *so that key tasks don't hinge on one person*

- ***Document core processes using SOPs*** *(fulfillment, customer service, vendor communications) so others can step in without guesswork*

- ***Use part-time or contract labor*** *during high-risk seasons to scale without overcommitting*

- ***Build a culture of responsiveness****, where employees understand the big picture and adapt quickly to new roles or systems*

Your team doesn't need to do everything. They just need to know what to do when circumstances change.

Key Takeaway: Resilience is a system of readiness. Businesses that survive turbulence are the ones that build *'shock absorbers'* into their operations *before* the road gets rough.

Why Agility Beats Size in Times of Crisis

Big businesses have volume, leverage, and access to large pools of capital. But they also have bureaucracy, slow decision-making, and long chains of command. In a stable economy, that might be fine. In a volatile one, it quickly becomes a liability.

This is where small businesses can win.

Agility—not size—is the real competitive advantage in a trade climate where prices shift overnight, supply lines break without warning, and customer expectations don't pause for global logistics problems.

Here's how to use agility to outmaneuver bigger players when it counts most.

Big Companies Move Slow. You Don't Have To.

Large corporations have layers of approvals, complex vendor contracts, and procurement teams that plan months (or even years) in advance. When conditions change fast (like a new tariff or shipping delay), they're often limited.

You're not.

As a small business, you can:

- *Switch suppliers in days, not quarters*

- *Adjust lead times, reorder volumes, or SKUs on the fly*

- *Test out new pricing or promotions this week, not six months from now*

- *Communicate changes directly to your customers without public relations teams, legal review or red tape*

In times of crisis, speed becomes more valuable than volume.

When disruption hits, the businesses that hesitate lose first. You don't need perfect data. You simply need clear visibility and the flexibility to act fast.

To operate with agility, be sure to keep a weekly pulse on your supplier capacity, shipping delays, and inventory levels. Also, make decisions at the level closest to the issue (often you, or a trusted operations manager). When establishing protocols or tactical operations, set thresholds that trigger action—like a 20% increase in freight rates, or a delay in key materials.

Quick decision-making doesn't mean recklessness. It means you're not waiting until it's too late to adjust course.

Pivot. Don't Panic.

Larger companies often have to double down on outdated plans because they've already sunk costs or made long-term contractual commitments. That's their weakness. Not yours.

Your strength is flexibility.

For example:

- *If a packaging supplier can't deliver, you can change the design, downgrade the insert, or switch to plain kraft and ship it.*

- *If raw material costs spike, you can test a domestic or local alternative—even if it means creating a smaller batch run.*

- *If a best-selling product becomes impossible to restock, you can bundle, discount, or relaunch it as a limited-time item rather than just going silent.*

These aren't *"Plan Bs."* They're how smart, nimble businesses stay profitable while others stall.

Agility Is a Customer Service Advantage

When supply chains fail, sadly, customer trust is often the first casualty. You risk losing both inventory and credibility. Agile businesses communicate clearly, shift expectations, and pivot without sounding like they're falling apart.

Be sure to:

- *Change shipping options quickly*

- *Send real-time updates on order statuses*

- *Replace products quickly or offer immediate alternatives*

- *Adjust pricing and value positioning in response to actual conditions, don't just provide a generic forecast*

In times of trade uncertainty, businesses that respond fast and communicate clearly look like leaders, even if they're the smallest players in the market.

Key Takeaway: Size gives you scale. Agility gives you control. Control is what customers crave. So, responsiveness is your biggest asset. Don't try to play a big company's game. Play the one you can win.

Flip Tariffs Into a Competitive Advantage

Did you know that while most businesses are treating tariffs like a threat, you can use them as leverage? During tariffs and trade disruptions, businesses commonly scramble to explain shortages, delays, and price hikes, but you can position your business as the one that saw it coming and built a strategy around it. Customers don't want excuses. They want reliability. And in uncertainty, consistency becomes a selling point.

Here's how to turn trade chaos into a competitive edge.

Lead With Stability

In times of disruption and chaos, being the calm voice matters. You don't have to pretend you're unaffected—you just need to demonstrate that you're prepared.

Example messaging:

> *"We're not experiencing delays because our suppliers are domestic."*

> *"You may see price hikes from our competitors, but our prices are stable through the season."*

"We've secured long-term inventory and fulfillment partnerships. No surprises here."

This isn't bragging. It's positioning.

Include Sourcing In Your Brand Story

Most businesses hide their sourcing strategy. You should highlight it, especially if you have diversified or localized your supply chain.

Include operational strength in your marketing language:

"Made in the U.S. means fewer delays, less markup, and faster shipping."

"We moved sourcing closer to home so you don't have to worry about trade uncertainty."

"No expensive overseas freight charges here. Just fast, direct-to-you service."

What others treat as hidden backend logistics, you can flaunt as front-end trust building.

Steal Customers from Unprepared Competitors

Every tariff or shipping delay causes a wave of customer frustration. That's your signal to swoop in and pounce. Have a strategy in place to gain additional leads and to steal customers from your competitors in times of turmoil.

For example, craft messaging that speaks directly to buyers burned by your competitors:

> *"Still waiting on backordered items from [big brand]? We're stocked and ready."*

> *"No international sourcing delays here—our fulfillment is handled stateside."*

> *"While others scramble, we've already adapted."*

When you're prepared and can adapt quickly, you can easily capitalize on their panic and turn their customers into your new prospect list.

Use PR and Advertising to Emphasize Readiness

The best time to stand out and differentiate your brand is when your competitors are quiet, apologizing, or behind schedule.

This is when you'll want to use every available channel—email, social, ads, and even press—to emphasize:

- *Inventory availability*

- *Faster fulfillment timelines*

- *Transparent pricing that isn't chasing tariff volatility*

When others are reacting to the latest headlines, you should be broadcasting that you've already anticipated and prepared for them.

Key Takeaway: Tariffs punish businesses that rely on the cheapest path. But they reward those who prepare for their impact. Smart sourcing and fast decision-making help you get ahead while others catch-up.

Lead With Confidence

Panic is contagious, but so is calm, decisive leadership. Trade uncertainty shakes up more than supply chains. It can quickly rattle leadership, teams, and customer trust. Businesses that hold their ground aren't just operationally and financially sound. They're clear, confident, and consistent in how they lead and communicate change.

If you've done the hard work—simplifying your product line, building resilient sourcing and protecting your cash flow—it's time to own that progress out loud. Confidence isn't noise. Its direction.

Here's how to lead from the front and bring your team and customers with you.

Explain Changes With Clarity, Not Apology

Prices change, shipping adjustments are needed, and products require updates. These aren't shortcomings if they're carried out with intention. Your customers and your team don't need perfection in times of chaos. They need clarity.

Here are some examples of clear, confident communication:

> *"We're shifting to domestic suppliers to avoid international freight delays."*

> *"Prices are changing to reflect the increased cost of materials, but your experience will stay consistent."*

> *"We've removed low-performing SKUs so we can ship your favorite products faster."*

Remember. Own your strategy. Don't just talk around it.

Include Operational Strategy Into Marketing Campaigns

Every logistical strength you've built can also double as a brand message. Don't assume customers know you're prepared for what's happening—tell them.

Here are some ways to integrate this into your marketing:

- *Email headlines:* *"How we're staying stocked while others scramble"*

- *Website banners:* *"Zero freight delays. Domestic inventory. Fast delivery."*

- *Product pages:* *"Made in the U.S. means no tariff markup, faster fulfillment."*

- *Social posts:* *"We're not out of stock. We planned ahead."*

Preparation is invisible until you talk about it.

Lead Your Team With Confidence and Candor

Within your organization, your team takes cues from your tone. If you seem uncertain or fearful, they will be too. If you act as if the sky is falling, morale and execution will mirror this sentiment.

Instead, be sure to openly share the strategy behind your decisions. When communicating statuses, keep the team updated on risks and pivots. Make sure that your management team welcomes employee input when it comes to brainstorming solutions, especially frontline staff. Finally, always recognize and celebrate wins (even small ones) when things go right, especially when the team is under pressure.

Confidence builds alignment. Transparency builds loyalty. When things feel chaotic, business leaders who speak calmly, deliver consistently, and stay engaged earn lasting trust.

Key Takeaway: Preparation works when people know about it. If you've put in the work, you have every reason to lead with confidence. Communicate early. Act like the one who saw it coming—because you did.

In the next chapter, we'll wrap up our discussion by focusing on long-term resilience. You'll learn how to spot when global trade turbulence is on the horizon, so that you can be proactive while the competition is reactive.

Chapter 8

How to Play the Long Game

T he reality of modern global trade requires that the most innovative businesses not just react to tariffs, but build logistical operations that can easily withstand them.

If the past few years have proven anything, it's this: *trade disruption isn't an isolated event . . . It's a recurring condition.* Unpredictable tariffs, export bans, port strikes, and raw material shortages are part of a new operating environment. You can't avoid these problems, but you can build a business that doesn't fall apart when they surface.

This chapter is about planning for longevity. This isn't just making it through the next round of import fees or freight increases. It's setting your business up so that tariffs, delays, and global tension become manageable, not mission critical.

Throughout the book, we've already discussed the *"hard parts:"* understanding risk, reacting to volatility, and cleaning up your supply chain. Now, it's time to focus on resilience by design.

Let's begin with the first move—rebuilding your value chain to start *"local first."*

Restructure Your Value Chain – "Local First"

If you want your business to survive trade wars, shipping delays, and tariff shocks, start by bringing your value chain closer to home. While not everything can be made locally, far more can than most business owners realize. And in an unpredictable trade climate, what matters most isn't cost. It's control.

Local-first thinking isn't about patriotism—it's about positioning. The shorter your supply lines, the faster you can respond to change. The closer your partners, the easier it is to maintain consistency, speed, and quality.

Let's rethink what *"local"* really means, and how to apply it in ways that strengthen your business.

What is a "Local Supplier?"

The term *"local"* doesn't mean that everything is made in your local neighborhood or state. It means building a solid value chain around suppliers, services, and partners that you can reach, verify, and rely on directly, within a certain region.

So, *"local suppliers"* might include:

- *Domestic manufacturers who produce products in smaller runs*

- *U.S.-based packaging or print vendors*

- *Local fulfillment centers or co-packers*

- *Nearby artisans or micro-producers who offer components or finishing services*

You don't need 100% localization. Even replacing a single international vendor with a reliable domestic one can significantly reduce your exposure.

Find What You Can, Where You Can

Start with high-risk, high-impact, or critical components like:

- *Raw materials with volatile international pricing (e.g., paper, textiles, metals)*

- *Packaging with long lead times or complex customization*

- *Components that rely on ports, air freight, or are subject to geopolitical bottlenecks*

Conduct a sourcing audit to answer the following questions:

- *"What part of this process do I **have** to import?"*

- *"What can I move local without losing quality or margin?"*

- *"What small-batch or flexible producers could I work with near me?"*

You're not looking for a perfect solution. You're just trying to reduce points of failure in your operation.

Partner With Local Producers and Finishers

More often than not, we don't think of the U.S. as a source of manufacturing. That's partly because we've been conditioned not to even look for domestic manufacturers. However, you might be surprised to find that there are small businesses within your state, or just a quick road trip away.

Even if you can't produce your entire product line locally, you still might be able to finish or assemble it locally.

For instance:

- *Import bulk ingredients or base materials, then mix, bottle, or package locally*

- *Print product labels, inserts, or sleeves near your fulfillment center*

- *Assemble kits or bundles with final touches applied by a domestic co-packer*

This allows you to preserve some elements of flexibility and speed, even if the raw materials come from overseas.

Use Local Fulfillment to Cut Lag and Risk

One of the secrets of Amazon's speed is its intricate network of fulfillment centers. This allows real-time adaptation of product demand. Similarly, you can localize **where** your product ships from, even if it's not 100% locally made.

Some options might include:

- *Regional 3PLs (third-party logistics) with multiple warehouse locations*

- *Micro-fulfillment hubs that batch and ship close to customer clusters*

- *Local courier partnerships that bypass national shipping congestion*

By reducing the physical distance between you and your customers, you cut transit risk, lead time, and customer frustration—even when global trade routes slow down.

Reframe "Local" as a Value Proposition

If you decide to use local production or fulfillment, don't hide it. Find a way to include it in your branding and marketing.

Transform the terms *"locally made," "locally fulfilled,"* or *"assembled in [City/State]"* into a visible and prominent part of your product story. Customers value speed and reliability, and they'll pay for it if they know what they're buying into.

Be sure to add this language to:

- *Product pages and inserts*

- *Your brand story (i.e., "About Us" page)*

- *Social content and "behind-the-scenes" photos*

- *Customer emails explaining product changes or improvements*

- *Sales presentations, videos, and customer inquiries*

Local-first isn't just a supply chain move. You should also view it as a UVP and marketing asset.

> **Key Takeaway:** You don't have to make everything domestically. Shorten the distance between your business and the team keeping it running. In turbulent times, a *"local-first"* mindset earns you speed, trust, and resilience.

U.S. / Mexico / Canada Nearshoring

Local sourcing is your first layer of defense against tariffs. Regional sourcing is your second.

As your business grows (or as certain materials or capacities are unavailable locally) you may need to look beyond the U.S., But that doesn't mean exclusively relying on global suppliers. It could mean looking next door.

Thanks to the United States-Mexico-Canada Agreement (USMCA)[1] drafted in 2020, nearshoring across North America gives small businesses access to reliable manufacturing and fulfillment without the same high exposure to overseas tariffs, freight delays, or geopolitical instability. When used strategi-

---

1. The USMCA substituted the North America Free Trade Agreement (NAFTA). For more information on the USMCA, see https://ustr.gov/trade-agreements/free-trade-agreements/united-stat es-mexico-canada-agreement

cally, it creates a balance between cost savings and operational control.

Nearshoring works best when you're ready to scale or diversify, but still want to stay out of harm's way.

Why Nearshoring Might Make Sense

Working with suppliers in Mexico or Canada can lower your production costs, shorten lead times, and reduce dependency on congested international ports. It also simplifies customs processes and offers stronger trade protections under USMCA than most overseas arrangements.

Mexico, for example, offers strong capacity in textiles, plastics, electronics assembly, and certain food and beverage sectors. Canada is known for high-quality printing, packaging, clean ingredient processing, and regulatory alignment for consumer goods. Both are easier to access by ground transportation, and although there has been some trade turbulence as of March 2025, this has settled down considerably as of the time of writing this book (i.e., May 2025).

How to Make Nearshoring Work

The key to successful nearshoring is preparation. Don't treat regional suppliers as just another *"cheap alternative"* to U.S. vendors. Treat them as an extension of your core value chain.

Start by identifying the parts of your operation where regional production could reduce cost or improve flexibility without increasing risk. Then, research manufacturers and logistics partners with a strong track record working with U.S.-based small businesses.

You'll want to ask the same questions you'd ask any local supplier:

- *How stable is their labor force?*

- *What's their average lead time?*

- *Do they offer transparent pricing?*

- *Can they grow with you?*

If your business is already shipping cross-border, it's worth evaluating whether dual-warehousing in the U.S. and Canada could reduce costs or speed up delivery.

And if you're shipping goods from a Mexican supplier, ensure your customs broker and freight partners are familiar with USMCA documentation requirements to reduce clearance delays.

Watch for Hidden Risks

As with any supplier, going regional does not guarantee a risk-free experience.

Labor instability, infrastructure breakdowns, and regional politics can still affect your supply chain—especially in parts of Mexico where industrial development has outpaced transportation capacity.

For example, the high demand for nearshoring and foreign investment is driving rapid development within key manufacturing and logistics hubs like Mexico City, Monterrey, and Guadalajara Mexico. However, the existing transportation network is struggling to keep up, often leading to congestion and inefficiencies.

It's also critical to account for currency fluctuations and regulatory requirements, especially if your product touches food, supplements, or skincare. That said, these risks are usually easier to spot, communicate around, and navigate around than in overseas, long-distance global relationships.

Build a Trade-Resilient Brand

When global trade is unstable and customers face delays, price hikes, or product shortages, companies that stand out aren't just the ones who deliver consistently—they're the ones who explain *why* they can deliver consistently. Operational stability is now a competitive advantage.

Your sourcing decisions, fulfillment speed, and inventory strategy all say something to your customers or prospects, whether you make it part of your core brand messaging or not.

Consumers today are paying closer attention to where products come from, how quickly they ship, and whether businesses are prepared for uncertainty. This means that preparedness is part of your brand story, whether you realize it or not.

If your competitors are constantly backordered or adjusting prices without explanation, this is your chance to stand apart with a fresh UVP (Unique Value Proposition).

Being trade-resilient means more than keeping products in stock. It also means showing your customers that you've built a business they can count on even when everything else is uncertain.

To start, focus on your language. Don't overpromise, but don't stay quiet either. If you've shifted production locally or even regionally, say so. If you've shortened delivery times while others are slipping, make that a part of your pitch to prospects.

Use phrases like *"Locally fulfilled," "Domestically produced,"* or *"Tariff-free supply chain"* in your website, product listings, email headers, sales inserts and customer onboarding flows.

If you've switched to regional vendors or redesigned your products to improve reliability, show that work in behind-the-scenes content. Post photos from your new vendor partnerships. Share why certain changes were made. Showcase the benefits—not just to you, but to the buyers as well.

This doesn't require flashy campaigns or lengthy explanations. It requires consistent messaging that says, *"We're not just selling stuff—we're planning ahead to serve you better than our competitors."*

Turn Resilience into Brand Confidence

When customers trust your business, they stop worrying about whether their order will ship on time. They stop second-guessing your prices. And they stop looking for alternatives.

You can earn that level of trust by being transparent with your changes, being clear about your values, and staying *proactive* when others are *reactive*. This type of confidence isn't built during a crisis. It's built years in advance and then validated under pressure. The more resilient your brand positioning, the more customer loyalty you'll earn.

Once your brand is known for rock-solid reliability, you can use that positioning to gain additional market share, expand into new product categories, pitch retail buyers, or launch B2B partnerships.

A brand known for consistency, fast delivery, and supplier integrity has more than just transactional value in the eyes of both suppliers and customers. A stellar reputation has the power to open doors with bigger vendors, reduces risk for collaborators, and makes you a preferred partner to work with in uncertain markets. That kind of brand equity is hard to replicate—and nearly impossible to fake.

> *Key Takeaway:* A trade-resilient brand is built on truth, not tactics. If you've worked hard to stabilize and streamline operations, talk about it. Your brand isn't just what you sell, it's what people know you can deliver.

Prepare for the Next Trade War Now

You might be wondering why I included this section. I mean, who's to say that there will be another trade war?

Well, the *next* trade war isn't a question of *if*. It's **when**.

Tariffs, import restrictions, supply bans, and political posturing are no longer historical outliers—they've become part of modern business cycles. You can't predict where trade challenges will come from, but you can start building a structure that responds faster, adapts better, and remains profitable when your competition is still figuring out what hit them.

Preparedness doesn't mean focusing on panic-driven decisions. It means giving your business more breathing room when the market tightens.

Here's how to create a plan you can rely on—before the news headlines make it necessary.

Adopt a Scenario-Based Planning Mindset

Start by sketching out three basic futures for your business:

- ***Best-case scenario:*** *Stable sourcing, minimal tariff changes, strong demand*

- ***Likely-case scenario:*** *Intermittent supply chain delays, moderate tariff increases, customer price sensitivity*

- ***Worst-case scenario:*** *High tariffs, export bans, major supplier collapse, market demand contraction*

Now ask yourself the tough questions:

- *"What would I do in each case?"*

- *"Where am I vulnerable?"*

- *"How can I be better prepared?"*

Use these answers to determine what needs to be built or put in place *now*, not when you're facing a crisis situation.

Create a Disruption Response Playbook

Every business should have a *"ready-to-go"* protocol in place when disruption hits.

This may include:

A documented list of backup suppliers (local, regional, and alternative material options)

An internal checklist for pausing low-performing SKUs, shifting lead times, or changing packaging

Pre-approved customer messaging you can deploy when shipments slow or costs rise

Financial fallback strategies like credit lines, cost-cutting levers, and cash preservation moves

The point here is that while everyone else is scrambling to figure out what to do, you'll already have a plan in motion.

Vet Your Vendors for Resilience

When working with new vendors and suppliers, you'll most likely need to start asking tougher questions:

"What's your plan if international shipping gets delayed by four weeks?"

"Does your company have multiple plants or just one point of failure?"

"Does your company stockpile critical inputs, or does it run 'just-in-time?'"

"Have you weathered past trade disruptions successfully?" "If so, how?"

Your vendors need to focus, not simply on fulfilling orders, but also on thinking and planning through disruption scenarios.

Strengthen Your Team's Flexibility

Make sure your team can respond without bottlenecks.

That means:

Cross-training key employees so tasks aren't missed when something shifts

Keeping critical decision-making close to the top so pivoting doesn't require excessive bureaucracy

Empowering frontline staff to communicate with customers clearly and quickly

Holding quarterly reviews of disruption readiness plans and adjusting based on market shifts

In a trade war, the speed of your internal alignment becomes your competitive edge.

Stay Up-to-Date Without Getting Overwhelmed

To stay up-to-date with current events, start by setting up a simple information pipeline:

Subscribe to trade updates from USTR, WTO, and your industry's trade publications

Follow logistics trends—especially shipping rates, port congestion, and customs updates

Keep an eye on geopolitical flashpoints (supply bans, sanctions, international talks)

You don't have to be policy analyst. But you definitely need to spot the warning signs before they start to affect your bottom line.

> **Key Takeaway:** Surviving the current disruption isn't enough. Your real edge comes from what you *build* between disruptions—systems that flex, vendors that hold, and decisions that don't stall.

The next trade war will reward the prepared. This is how you make sure you're one of them.

The Final Takeaway: Stay Lean. Stay Local. Stay Ready.

Global trade isn't getting simpler. It's getting more unstable, more political, and more expensive to ignore. But you don't have to play defense forever. The strategies in this book are designed to help you shift from a reaction-based mindset to one of clarity and control, all while building a business that can operate confidently no matter what happens overseas.

Here's what you now have:

- *A clear understanding of how tariffs and supply chain friction affect small businesses*

- *Practical strategies for shifting sourcing closer to home*

- *Tools for reducing your dependency on unstable suppliers or regions*

- *Guidance for protecting your margins without cutting corners*

- *A framework for long-term resilience—one that puts speed, trust, and control back in your hands*

You don't need perfect timing or perfect forecasts. You need a business that bends without breaking. So, the next time tariffs spike, ports close, or a supplier disappears—you won't get caught off guard.

You'll be ready.

And that, is what a tariff-proof business looks like.

Did This Book Help You?

If this book helped you rethink your sourcing strategy or feel more prepared, I'd be forever grateful if you take a moment to leave a review. Your feedback doesn't just help authors like me. It helps other business owners find the tools they need to adapt, stay competitive, and thrive, no matter what the global economy throws their way.

Please leave a review on Amazon or your favorite retailer and let others know why this book matters, and how it can help them too.

Thanks again for reading.

With Love and Gratitude,

Donovan Garett

Appendix A - Emerging Markets

As global supply chains continue to shift, more business owners are asking the same question: *Are there untapped manufacturing opportunities in places like Nigeria, Kenya, or Bangladesh—and are they worth pursuing?*

The answer is: *possibly, but not without caution.*

Emerging markets often offer lower labor costs and fewer barriers to entry when compared to more established regions. But those potential savings can be quickly wiped out by political instability, unreliable infrastructure, or inconsistent enforcement of contracts.

I decided to include this mini-guide to provide you with a practical lens to evaluate whether sourcing from an emerging market fits into your broader supply strategy, or whether the risks outweigh the savings.

Why Emerging Markets Are Getting Attention

As tariffs rise in countries like China and trade tensions start to spill into North America, small businesses are forced to look outside the traditional sourcing map.

Countries like Nigeria, Ghana, Kenya, as well as parts of Southeast Asia and Eastern Europe are now positioning themselves as manufacturing alternatives for small and mid-sized global partners. Local governments are encouraging foreign partnerships, regional trade blocs are expanding, and a new generation of producers is hungry for international contracts.

These markets are especially appealing for:

- *Textiles, leather goods, and apparel*

- *Handcrafted or artisanal consumer products*

- *Basic manufacturing with low automation requirements*

- *First-mover advantage in underdeveloped categories*

But low cost doesn't mean low risk—and that's where most small businesses get caught.

Lower Labor and Production Costs

In many of these countries, labor costs are significantly below those of Asia or Latin America. For labor-intensive industries like garment production or assembly, the potential savings can add up quickly.

Less Competition, More Flexibility

In many lesser-known regions, you're not just one of a thousand clients. Smaller manufacturers in these markets are often more willing to negotiate flexible MOQs, collaborate on product development, or customize production to meet your specs.

Access to Regional Trade Networks

Some emerging economies are part of larger trade blocs—like ECOWAS (West Africa), EAC (East Africa), or the AfCFTA (African Continental Free Trade Area)—that can create access to multiple markets through one supplier.

https://www.ecowas.int

https://www.eac.int/

https://au-afcfta.org/

When Emerging Markets Might Make Sense

You should consider sourcing from an emerging market when:

*You have **non-critical SKUs** you can test in small batches*

*You're building a **long-term relationship** with a specific region or supplier you trust*

*You have a **logistics partner or agent** on the ground to manage production and quality*

*The **product category aligns** with the country's natural strengths (e.g., leather from Nigeria, woven textiles from Kenya)*

Do **not** depend on an emerging-market supplier for your most time-sensitive, high-volume, or complex product categories—at least not without significant safeguards in place.

Risks to Watch For

Political and Economic Instability

Countries like Nigeria have strong entrepreneurial ecosystems but also face recurring political uncertainty, foreign exchange restrictions, and infrastructure breakdowns. A nationwide strike, power grid failure, or election cycle can derail or stop operations overnight.

Poor Infrastructure and Logistics

Reliable roadways, ports, internet, and consistent electricity are not guaranteed. This can be especially troublesome during the rainy season and climate instability. Delays in shipping, customs clearance, or even internet-based communication can turn a 30-day production schedule into 90+ days without warning.

Limited Contract Enforcement

Even with a written agreement, enforcement in certain jurisdictions may be difficult or impossible. If something goes wrong, you may have no realistic legal recourse without an expensive and drawn-out international dispute.

Quality Control and Standards

Factories may not be ISO-certified or familiar with Western expectations around compliance, documentation, or quality inspection. You'll need to build in time and budget for quality control and multiple rounds of sampling.

How to Reduce the Risk

Here are some tips to mitigate risks when dealing with partners within Emerging Markets:

*Start with **a single product or prototype**, not your full line*

*Communicate using **clear documentation and visual references**—don't rely on assumptions*

*Use **escrow or staged payments** instead of large upfront deposits*

*Conduct **third-party inspections** before goods ship*

*Work with **international freight partners** that understand customs, documentation, and insurance in the country of origin*

Be prepared for delays and build them into your planning

The Bottom Line on Emerging Markets

Emerging markets can offer real cost advantages, but they come with real operational risks. This isn't a quick fix for your sourcing problems. It's a long-term play that requires patience, due diligence, and the willingness to navigate ambiguity.

For small business owners who approach it strategically, with clear expectations and strong safeguards—these markets may become part of a diversified sourcing plan from regions that your competition might miss.

But if you're relying on them to rescue your margins without a backup plan in place, you may be risking more headaches.

P.S. — I'm currently working on a quick reference cheatsheet that lists over 20 countries that qualify as Emerging Markets, along with their key industries, natural resources and labor capacity. If you'd like a copy, please email me at DonovanGarett Media@gmail.com

Appendix B - How to Use ABC Inventory Analysis

N ot all inventory is created equal. Some products move quickly and drive revenue. Others take up space, tie up cash, and collect dust. ABC inventory analysis is a simple way to sort your stock based on value and sales impact—so you can make smarter decisions about what to protect, what to reorder, and what to let go.

Here's how it works:

A Items – Your most valuable products

Typically make up ~20% of your SKUs

Generate ~70–80% of your total revenue

*Require **tight control** and regular monitoring*

*Ideal for **safety stock**, fast reordering, and prioritizing suppliers*

B Items – Mid-tier performers

Make up ~30% of your SKUs

Contribute ~15–25% of your total revenue

Need moderate attention

Good candidates for periodic reordering and promotional bundling

C Items – Low-value or slow movers

Often ~50% of your SKUs

Account for less than 10% of total revenue

Can be phased out, discounted, or only restocked as needed

Why it matters: When supply chains get tight or cash is limited, you can't afford to treat every SKU the same. ABC analysis tells you what to prioritize—and what to let go—so you're protecting what actually moves the needle.

ABC inventory analysis isn't just a tool for prioritizing re-orders. It's a powerful decision-making framework for clearing out slow-moving inventory strategically without damaging your margins or diluting brand value.

Here's how you might use ABC inventory analysis to decide which items to discount (and how deeply):

How To Decide What to Discount

Step 1: Categorize Your Inventory

Start by running a basic ABC analysis using sales volume and revenue contribution.

- **A Items** = Top sellers with strong margins

- **B Items** = Mid-tier performers

- **C Items** = Low-turnover, low-revenue products—your slow movers

C items are where most dead weight lives.

Step 2: Evaluate Inventory Age and Holding Costs

For **C items**, ask:

- *"How long have they been sitting in storage?"*

- *"Are they seasonal or outdated?"*

- *"Are they taking up space better used for faster-moving A or B items?"*

- *"Are they costing you money in storage, insurance, or fulfillment inefficiencies?"*

If a product hasn't moved in 90+ days and isn't forecasted to rebound, it's a drain on resources—not an asset.

Step 3: Decide on a Discount Strategy by Category

C Items:

- Mark down aggressively (30–50% or more) to liquidate

- Bundle with A or B items to increase perceived value

- Use for promotions, gift-with-purchase, or subscriber rewards

- Consider listing on third-party liquidation platforms if direct sales fail

B Items:

- Discount moderately (10–20%) during sales cycles

- Test bundling or re-pricing before writing off

- Consider product upgrades or simplification rather than elimination

A Items:

- Rarely discounted unless part of a high-visibility campaign

- Focus on maintaining margin and stock continuity

- May benefit from price increases or limited-time premium versions

Step 4: Use Data to Prevent Future Overstock

Once you've cleared out slow movers, prevent the problem from recurring:

Reduce purchase frequency or order size for similar C-class SKUs

Test small batches before scaling up any new B or C item

Focus most of your reordering budget on A-class products that actually drive revenue

Final Rule of Thumb

Discount to regain space and cash. Don't just mark down items to stay busy. If a product isn't serving your customers or your bottom line, it's not worth keeping around at any price.

8 Mistakes to Avoid

1. Only Looking at Sales Volume, Not Profitability

The mistake: Categorizing products based on how often they sell—but ignoring how much profit they generate. **Fix it:** Sort inventory by revenue contribution or gross margin, not just units sold.

2. Treating ABC Categories as Static

The mistake: Running analysis once and assuming it holds forever. **Fix it:** Reassess your ABC categories quarterly or after any major market shift. Products rise and fall in importance.

3. Over-ordering C Items Just to "Have Variety"

The mistake: Keeping too many slow movers in stock to fill shelves or offer choice. **Fix it:** C items should be discounted, bundled, or retired—not reordered unless they serve a specific purpose (e.g., seasonal, niche audience).

4. Over-relying on *"Gut Feel,"* not customer-driven data

The mistake: Letting emotion or attachment to a product override data (e.g., *"But customers love that one!"*). **Fix it:** Use objective sales data—not memory or assumptions—to classify SKUs.

5. Not Tying ABC Insights to Operational Decisions

The mistake: Running the analysis but not acting on it (e.g., still restocking every SKU equally). **Fix it:** Use ABC categories to prioritize reorders, adjust safety stock, plan promotions, and streamline SKUs.

6. Ignoring Inventory Holding Costs

The mistake: Forgetting that space, insurance, and management cost money—even for items that *"might sell eventually."* **Fix it:** Weigh the **cost of holding** slow-moving inventory against the potential revenue it brings in.

7. Misclassifying High-Value, Low-Volume Products

The mistake: Classifying premium products as C items because they sell less frequently. **Fix it:** Look at revenue or margin contribution, not just units sold. A slow seller might still be worth keeping if it carries a strong profit margin or strategic value.

8. Not Using ABC to Guide Purchasing Behavior

The mistake: Buying everything in bulk without regard to sales behavior. **Fix it:** Order A items more frequently in larger quantities, and order C items conservatively—or not at all.

Appendix C - Financial Diligence and Vetting Partners

DISCLAIMER: Let me start by stating that I am not a lawyer. This is not legal advice. Before signing any contracts or other documentation, please always consult a qualified attorney — especially when dealing with freight, intellectual property or any other sensitive matter.

With that out of the way, I wanted to include a brief checklist that may help you begin your research when vetting a new U.S. supplier. Most of these sources are freely available via your local (or county) library, and can prove helpful in cutting through the noise and determining whether a supplier is worth investing in long-term.

Why is this so important?

Because you're not just choosing a supplier—you're choosing a risk exposure. If your manufacturer goes out of business, fails to deliver, or suddenly stops communicating, it doesn't matter how cheap or close they were. *You will lose precious time, money, and credibility*.

Here's where to look:

Search for UCC Filings

What is a Uniform Commercial Code (UCC) search?

It's a process of reviewing public records to identify liens or security interests filed against a debtor's assets, providing insight into the debtor's financial health and potential creditors. These liens are filed as UCC-1 statements with the state's Secretary of State office, acting as public notice of a creditor's interest in the collateral. [1]

Where to look:

- *Your state's Secretary of State website; or*

- *a UCC search portal like https://debanked.com/free-ucc -search/*

What it tells you: *If the business has pledged its inventory, equipment, or receivables as collateral for loans.*

Multiple active UCC filings *can indicate debt load or liquidity stress.*

Recent filings *may suggest new borrowing—possibly to stay afloat.*

---

1. For more information, see the National Association of Secretaries of State at https://www.nass.org/ or your state's Secretary of State homepage.

A single UCC filing isn't a red flag. Several filings from multiple lenders might be.

Check Court Records for Lawsuits, Judgments, or Bankruptcy

Where to look:

- PACER (federal court records) – https://pacer.uscourts.gov

- Local and state court portals

Sites like:

- Justia — https://www.justia.com/

- DocketBird — https://www.docketbird.com/

- Court Listener — https://www.courtlistener.com/

What to look for:

- Recent breach-of-contract claims

- Supplier disputes with other clients

- Bankruptcy filings (especially under Chapter 11 or 7)

Why it matters: A history of disputes or financial distress may foreshadow delayed shipments, missed deadlines, or unreliable service.

Ask for Proof of Business Insurance

This should be a non-negotiable request. A financially stable manufacturer should carry:

- **General liability insurance**

- **Product liability insurance**

- Optional: **Business Interruption insurance**

You don't need to read every clause—just verify that coverage exists and is active. This can protect you if something goes wrong (e.g., damaged goods, on-site accidents, fire).

Consider Payment Terms as a Signal

A supplier demanding **100% payment upfront** for every order may have cash flow issues.

A supplier willing to offer **net-15 or net-30 terms** likely has more financial breathing room and trust in their operation.

Request tiered terms (e.g., 50% down, 50% on delivery) if you're new—this reduces your risk and tests their reliability.

Gauge Transparency During Conversations

When you ask about capacity, equipment, staffing, or cash flow management:

A confident, detailed answer suggests control and competence.

Vague responses, deflection, or irritation may point to underlying issues.

Sample question: *"Have you made any recent capital investments or expanded production capacity in the past year?"*

Remember: This isn't prying—it's professional diligence.

Online Business Directories and Review Platforms

Be sure to check:

Better Business Bureau (BBB) for unresolved complaints

Glassdoor (for employee sentiment—turnover can reflect instability)

LinkedIn (is the company growing, hiring, or shrinking?)

Even a lack of online presence can be telling in today's market.

If you have industry contacts, pick up the phone and ask about the supplier.

Appendix D - Canada, Mexico, U.K. and Australian Resources

This appendix is to provide non-U.S. business owners (specifically in **Canada, Mexico, the United Kingdom, and Australia)** with guidance on finding domestic suppliers and reducing reliance on international imports.

Canada

Platforms and Directories

Canadian Company Capabilities (CCC) – a government-maintained directory for manufacturers and service providers. https://www.ic.gc.ca

Made in Canada Directory – features Canadian-made products and suppliers. https://madeinca.ca

Manufacturing.ca – National industry directory for B2B connections. https://www.n49.com/search/manufacturing/1/canada/

Local Chambers of Commerce – Business directories and regional matchmaking.

Support Programs

Innovation, Science and Economic Development (ISED) grants — https://ised-isde.canada.ca/site/ised/en

Export Development Canada (EDC) resources — https://www.edc.ca/

Provincial economic development programs (e.g., Ontario Made, Alberta Innovates) — https://www.investcanada.ca/programs-incentives

Mexico

Platforms and Directories

ProMéxico *(now integrated into Secretaría de Economía)* – Government portal for industrial data, supplier matching, and trade support. https://www.gob.mx/se

Mexico Business Directory – Private B2B directory for manufacturers and logistics. https://www.kompass.com/z/mx/r/mexico/mx_1818/

Index Nacional (Maquiladora Association) – Contacts and support for export manufacturing companies. https://index.org.mx/about-us/

Canacintra (National Chamber of the Transformation Industry) – Manufacturing contacts across sectors. https://portal.canacintra.org.mx/sectores/

Support Programs

Government-backed supplier development programs — https://www.proyectosmexico.gob.mx/en/home/

Regional economic development offices and trade promotion agencies — https://www.gob.mx/

Public-private accelerators focused on domestic capability building — https://incubamas.com/https://startupmexico.com/

United Kingdom

Platforms and Directories

Made in Britain – Directory and badge program promoting UK-made products. https://www.madeinbritain.org

UKTI Supplier Database *(via Department for Business and Trade)* – B2B export and supplier matching. https://www.great.gov.uk

The Manufacturer Directory – Listings of UK-based industrial and consumer product manufacturers. https://makeitbritish.co.uk/, https://www.qimtek.co.uk/uk-manufacturing-engineering-directory, https://uk-md.co.uk/

Chambers of Commerce UK Network – Local sourcing and networking options. https://www.britishchambers.org.uk/

Support Programs

UK Export Finance programs for UK-based production — https://www.ukexportfinance.gov.uk/

Innovate UK and regional growth hubs — https://ukinnovationhub.ukri.org/

Local enterprise partnerships (LEPs) offering sourcing and production grants — https://www.visitbritain.org/resources-destination-partners/working-local-enterprise-partnerships-leps

Australia

Platforms and Directories

Industry Capability Network (ICN) – Australia's primary manufacturing and sourcing portal. https://gateway.icn.org.au

AusIndustry – Supplier programs, manufacturing grants, and business matching. https://business.gov.au

Australian Made Campaign – Directory and certification for local products. https://australianmade.com.au/

Support Programs

Modern Manufacturing Initiative (MMI) and state-level grants — https://business.gov.au/grants-and-programs/modern-manufacturing-initiative-manufacturing-integration

Regional Development Australia (RDA) resources — https://www.rda.gov.au/

Advanced Manufacturing Growth Centre (AMGC) projects and partner networks — https://www.amgc.org.au/

www.ingramcontent.com/pod-product-compliance
Lightning Source LLC
Chambersburg PA
CBHW022132080426
42734CB00006B/326

9 7 8 1 9 6 3 2 6 7 3 5 8